~getting away with everything

Unlikely Books
www.UnlikelyStories.org
New Orleans, Louisiana

~getting away with everything

Copyright © 2020-21 Vincent A. Cellucci and Christopher Shipman
Cover collages Copyright © 2021 Christopher Shipman
Cover design Copyright © 2021 Vincent A. Cellucci
Book design Copyright © 2021 Vincent A. Cellucci and Unlikely Books

All Rights Reserved

Twenty Dollars US

ISBN: 978-1-7337143-8-9

Library of Congress Control Number: 2021945461

Unlikely Books
www.UnlikelyStories.org
New Orleans, Louisiana

"This single poem by a double poet is one of lament and elegy, a hymn to a lost place (New Orleans) and to a lost life (pre-Covid), but it is also a song of exuberance and hope, a conversation about loss that yet celebrates the possibility of conversation. The two poets, who are not distinguished by any textual markers, speak themselves in multiple registers, ranging from the intensely personal to the broadly social and political, so the effect is ultimately of a round of voices alternating and overlapping. Entertaining, uplifting, and brilliant. And if you lose track of who that "I" is referring to at any given moment, ask if you're all that certain when you say it yourself."

—**Bill Lavender**, author of *My ID* and *Three Letters*

"The bad boys of poetry are back! In this second collaboration we see Vincent Cellucci and Christopher Shipman still enjoying their high jinx, surprising metaphors, attention to sound and deep investment in place. But they also have grown and deepened; the "former reprobates" now take on fatherhood, jobs, moving, and aging. *~getting away with everything* is an immensely lively book."

—**Beth Ann Fennelly**, author of *Heating & Cooling: 52 Micro-Memoirs*

"*~getting away with everything* is a collection of comings and goings but also what staying entails. Shipman and Cellucci come together seamlessly in this series that is a long series of breaks. This is a book that reaches down into the depths of deep song and works its way towards what I call deep reflection. These poems are mirrors and windows into what once was and who one once was. The poems look back and show what kind of potential there is in the sentimental and how not all nostalgia is naive and positive. Instead, the pieces crack open the moments for investigation and apply thought and feeling to experience in tragic and maybe dark romantic ways, but their eyes are always on what might come next."

—**Kenning JP García**, author of *So This Is Story*

Publisher's Preface
by Jonathan Penton

Badass poets Vincent A. Cellucci and Christopher Shipman are back, with an exhilarating, invigorating, and extremely long book of free verse, ~*getting away with everything* (~*gawe*). I've spent many happy months now, editing this massive tome, and it's time to sit down to write the preface. I've drafted it a dozen times trying to capture the wildness of the book, and each time I sit down to write, the preface grows a little less ecstatic, a little more melancholy.

Towards the end of 2013, Unlikely Books received an unsolicited submission, _a ship on the line (_asotl), from Cellucci and Shipman. Shipman lived in New Orleans, and Cellucci lived in Baton Rouge, Louisiana, about 80 miles west of New Orleans. They had previously run a reading series, The River Writers, in Baton Rouge together, and when they passed that on, they began a poetic collaboration that has now lasted almost a decade. _asotl was a sort of correspondence between Cellucci and Shipman. It was, like their reading series, focused on the Mississippi River, both literally and as muse, as backdrop and connection between the authors.

At the time, Unlikely Books was a two-person outfit; Michelle Greenblatt, living outside of Fort Lauderdale, Florida, and myself, living in the small city of Lafayette, Louisiana, about 130 miles west of New Orleans. Greenblatt saw the manuscript first, fell in love with it, and immediately chose for Unlikely Books to publish it. In the Unlikely way, she worked intimately with Cellucci and Shipman, forming what I believe to be the best possible version of _asotl. _asotl was published in August 2014, and named as a finalist for the Eric Hoffer Book Award.

In autumn of 2014, I edited, and Unlikely Books published, Greenblatt's massive poetic tome, *ASHES AND SEEDS*. It is, to put it mildly, irregular for a press to publish a staffer's book. But as Greenblatt's illness advanced, we felt we needed to release the book promptly, and she trusted me to edit it.

    We planned a series of joint book release parties for _asotl and *ASHES AND SEEDS*: four readings in New Orleans, Baton Rouge, and Lafayette starring Cellucci, Shipman, and Greenblatt. Everything was set and ready to go until November 3 of that year, when the state of Florida cut Greenblatt's pain medication. She found herself unable to handle car rides, let alone a plane trip and a week of intense traveling and reading. Devastated, she cancelled her trip to Louisiana.

    Trying to make the best of it, Greenblatt made a video. Assisted by her partner, Kyle Ramsay, she made a 20-minute presentation, in her garage, reading from *ASHES*. She was in significant pain when she did so, and it was obvious. Shipman, Cellucci and I grabbed her presentation and a big-screen television, and fueled by alcohol, frustration, extension cords, and enormous pride in the two books, we zipped across south Louisiana, finding delight in the work and rage for the state of Florida's health care system.

    Greenblatt died October 19, 2015. I became Unlikely Books's sole publisher and editor, working with some regular freelance designers and copy editors. In the meantime, Cellucci, Shipman, and I grew close, making regular plans to meet in various Louisiana cities to read poetry, drink, and celebrate our creative friendship and continuing existence. We traveled around the US for book fairs and conferences together, engaging in embarrassing acts of vandalism and regular bouts of debauchery. But in 2018, Shipman and his wife found work in Greensboro, North Carolina, and left New Orleans, hoping to secure better financial opportunities and a better education for their daughter. In 2019, Cellucci's partner got her dream job at the Delft University of Technology, in the Netherlands. Given the worsening American political climate, Cellucci felt compelled to become an expatriate, and when he found work at the Delft University library, they decided to emigrate. They sold their house and left the States, with plans to permanently relocate to Europe. *~getting away with everything* begins with these departures.

~*gawe* was written mostly during the 2020 lockdown, and tells the story of two people who survived. They did not survive because they are "survivors," or heroes, or because of any intrinsic characteristic or virtue on their parts. Cellucci and Shipman are white, straight, good-looking men in their thirties, with all the privilege that implies. Beyond this, they are simply lucky.

Beginning with the title, which the authors spin and riff on throughout the book, ~*gawe* meticulously chronicles their good fortune, both their joy while living in Louisiana and their optimism upon leaving. Though it is not told in chronological order, the book has a narrative structure: they consider New Orleans, they leave the area, and they try to find their way in new environments. As poets, they explore every step of their geographical and emotional journeys.

In some ways, _*asotl* and ~*gawe* are part of a single, continuous poetic thread. Their creation was simple enough. Shipman woke up first, wrote a poem, and sent it to Cellucci. Cellucci woke up, read it, and wrote a poem in response. He sent his poem to Shipman, who wrote his own response. This pattern has continued for almost a decade, now (though time zones have caused the order of production to reverse). But when reading these books, don't assume you know what was written by whom. Some poems offer straightforward details of the author's life, revealing his identity. In many more, the author's identity is slippery, and the poems do not necessarily appear in the order in which they were written. As poet and publisher Bill Lavender says about ~*gawe*, "And if you lose track of who that 'I' is referring to at any given moment, ask if you're all that certain when you say it yourself." On one level, this book is two distinct and different stories. On another, it is the deliberate intersection and melding of those stories. The result is a tale that is archetypical and epic: the survivor in flight, identity unspecified. New Orleans is a famously romantic place, an exciting backdrop for stories of exodus. But the themes of ~*gawe* are ultimately not dependent on its environments. Many of us have felt, at some point, obliged to leave our homes, and these sorts of personal journeys are at the heart of ~*gawe*. The book has a strong sense of place, but is not about Louisiana, North

Carolina, or the Netherlands, but about endings, beginnings, and the ever-present risk and reality of flight.

_asotl is a highly symbolic, somewhat abstract book. It revolves around a wistfulness that never experiences direct description or definition. In _asotl, Cellucci and Shipman's Mississippi River sweeps through their individual and shared memories, offering focus, but no succor, for their ambivalent relationship with their past and present.

~gawe, with its narrative nature, is highly accessible by comparison. It opens with a fearful prayer for New Orleans—that perpetually doomed city—but moves quickly into details of the authors' doomed lives there, and the necessity of their personal exoduses (and the exoduses of lyrical narrative). Cellucci himself was displaced from New Orleans during Katrina, thus living in Baton Rouge from 2005-2019. Although ~gawe is informed by Louisiana's major struggles, it focuses on the personal reasons Cellucci and Shipman left the area—the emotional factors which precipitated those decisions. As anti-poet Kenning JP Garcia says about the book, "not all nostalgia is naive and positive." There's a lot of homesickness in this book, a longing for a place which is fundamentally bad for our authors. With curiosity and insight, Cellucci and Shipman consider their stories—their new environments and their memories of south Louisiana, page after thoughtful page.

Nostalgia, positive or negative, does not slow life down. In 2016, my partner and I moved from Lafayette to New Orleans; in 2020, we held a pandemic wedding on the banks of the Mississippi. In the spring of 2021, Cellucci and his partner had a child. I write this in August 2021, as the Delta Variant erases the progress that New Orleans had made against covid. I miss Michelle Greenblatt, who should be writing this preface. I miss my friends Vincent and Christopher. They both hope to come back to New Orleans in October, for this book's release party, but who knows when Cellucci and his family will be able to safely travel back and forth from the EU, and domestic travel now seems equally daunting.

I've read ~*gawe* a dozen times now, and each time it asks me: *what do we do with regret?* ~*gawe* is written against a backdrop of loss: to Katrina, to Louisiana's vanishing coastline, to covid, to other illness. Searching for emotional utility in such circumstances, it looks both forward, and eternally backward—finding tragedy, grief, and the joyous specter of emotional freedom.

So I read, and re-read, this book with a sense of gratitude, for all that such a well-layered book of poetry can offer. To read _*a ship on the line* and ~*getting away with everything* is to watch our authors process their senses of longing and loss. It is to feel the texture and see the shapes of their sadnesses. I consistently find that such observations bring me greater insight into my own experiences with survival and flight.

the order in which they appear

publisher's preface by Jonathan Penton   5

I. opening words like floodgates
Solastalgia   23
Time Travel   26
ghosts in tow   28
This Morning   31
some mornings   34
Nightlight   36
porch sharks   38
Any Poem about Any River   40
sometimes stars are sharks   43

II. a pilgrimage to the fountain of nothing
precarious nothings   47
Lately   49
air mail   51
getaway cars   54
Chthonic Sheet of Ice   60
chronic chthonic disorder   62
Past the Night   64
swallowing spit   68
On the Morning of My 37th Birthday   70
my blur flew from puddle to puddle   75
my ghost flew from city to country   78
sweeping et al.   80
chess pieces untidily scattered   83
okay, boomer   84

III. churn the earth

Jack's Ashes	87
alt burial rites	94
gonna set your flag on fire	96
Too Dark to Tell	99
Measurements	101

IV. this never-ending theater

everything possible	107
groping for consent	108
Normal Stranger Ogling Octopus	111
negative capability	113
two enemas down / one to go	114
Here Comes the Rain	116
roaring an oath to rainclouds	119
grand slam	120
missing booth inside your head	121
In the Wake of Chthonic Fires	124
lost tops	126
Said the Night at Intermission	128
I pour a fancy beer in a cheap glass	131

V. undeserving of further resolve

Family Reunion at the Hunting Lodge	135
Snaggletooth	137
to turn the other cheek	141
disinvited to the soulless sugar-coated banality of the average family day outing	143
lurking in the glow	144

drive thru confessional, unframed	145
nederland alternative endings	147
another city lights pilgrimage	150
moped morse code	156
Porch Beers VS. the Bore of Existential Fears	158

VI. the dampest of spirits

one puddle	163
Now When I am	166
stations of the crossed	170
The New Human Within	173
roaming free blues / a systemic murder ballad	174
Unrepentant Caverns	177
sacred in sacred out	180
Will the Real Secret Agent Please Stand Up?	183
mae's-en-scène	185
I'm the Kingpin in the City of My Sad Song	196
honestly	198
street food nude	199
Sharing a Smoke	202
northern high noon	204
The Obligation to Meaning	206
raised as a barrel in the cellar	208
The New Bird Sings	211
one last hurricane party in nc	213

VII. living past the invisible

corona cooler	217
Spring Quarantine	220

ride again	225
The News on the Corner	227
follow the yellow bit inroad	230
on my 37th year and yet another day around the sun	234
An American Vigil	236
wounded soldier	240
acknowledgments	243
shout-outs	244
about the authors	245
other titles by Vincent A. Cellucci ~ Christopher Shipman	246
recent titles from Unlikely Books	247

~getting

away

with

everything

Dedicated to the memory of our editor, friend and fellow Unlikely, Michelle Greenblatt

Everything is not enough
And nothin' is too much to bear
Where you been is good and gone
All you keep's the getting there

—Townes van Zandt, "To Live Is to Fly"

We tell ourselves stories in order to live...

—Joan Didion, *The White Album*

I. OPENING WORDS LIKE FLOODGATES

Solastalgia

We would come out of the floodgates and my dad would say, 'Head for the lemon trees!' [...] The older folks always discouraged us from going, out of respect. The legend goes that you were always to bring some kind of sacrifice. So, somebody left some lemons for the ancestors. [...] But now that it's washing away [...] it needs to be seen before it gets lost.

—Richie Blink from "Louisiana's Disappearing Coast Takes Ancient History With It." 89.9, WWNO. New Orleans Public Radio

It's easy to imagine
                                        Richie Blink
                                        on the radio

unblinking
        when he cants   opening words

            like *floodgates*
            or *my dad*.

And when he says   *say*
then *lemon trees*   something

as simple as   *going*   really goes.

It's even easier to conjure
the young ones   squinting at the sun

        soliciting spirits alive in the blood
            the old folk left

when he says   *respect*
or *sacrifice*.

But when *legend*   slips out
of his mouth

it sounds like ancestor   like *washed*
away   like *lost*.

I say   selfishly   before the final island

disappears
                               let's tell a story—
every story of home—
that lives in the static on every station.

Let's get away   with everything
while we're still slow   in the process

of disappearing.

Let's head for the lemon trees   pluck
the fruit pluck yesterday
                          pluck
ancient history   pluck   today.

      In that distance the past glistens—
        a floating house shaping

                its own shore

the way an opened letter
tucked in a drawer in a previous life

        wants another tongue.

Yesterday's splintered limbs say

don't let this be the last memory of me
        head for the trees

        make an offering.

    If the waves lap at the door
            let us swim.

If the sky is never finished

        nothing is.

Time Travel

Two hours to the mountains, four to the sea.

That's what people who knew North Carolina kept saying
about Greensboro. The move from New Orleans
was a number of hours hard to recall.

For a haul that long you can't count time but space—
hours replaced with miles. Around 800, give or take.

It was a hotel halfway, just past Atlanta. A 15ft U-Haul
with hatchback in tow. It was walkie-talkies—
a finger on talk. It was worry

for the woman and kid out in front
barely cresting every hill in our dying Nissan.

I never let them escape my sight, my square of windshield
like a rented world, but they always felt far away.

Maybe moving anywhere would feel far away
after 12 years in Louisiana; after Mardi Gras
masquerading as rain and wind; after king cakes,
sin, and saints splayed on every table;

after the birth of a kid, a near divorce—what people call
beginning again.

On the road I remembered how, in grad school
in Baton Rouge, when I'd go home to Arkansas
it was always as they say: everything seemed small.

But smaller than that—like I could never go back.

Because the moment I left the place it had already gone—
disappeared into dream. I knew then
I'd surrender sleep to remember waking.

Now we're waking up in Greensboro. We had to get used
to the hour difference, but that didn't take long.

We're looking forward to the mountains.

And when we're ready for the four-hour trek
to walk along the beach—all our exhausted ghosts in tow
pretending to be innocent shadows.

ghosts in tow

I gotta steam burn
making tropical tea
for nobody and me

same doom
different poem

I wanna leave too
how she stormed off   to her room

                how we storm
                          home

getting drunk's
still fun
so's gravity

stay alive
look alive
on the ball court or beach or empty lot

it's a turtle eat
turtle fuck
terrarium
    out there
      —in here—

kevlar shell breast

                however remember   follow snakes
                        stay wild
                                get away
                            alive
                                getty up
                        all night
                                alerts
                    let her riff

        nobody knows
                    my troublesome names
        like you
            you see

my ex called me
a loadie faery
and well

I usually do pack a lil
heat & peat
    offerings for those that don't get to

hoot for the undergod
that takes it all away

that may   tap into truth
but I don't hold onto shit
putting ice cubes
in my veuve clicq

eating stuffed crust
on a virtual porch
no one has to shovel
the bottles off of
tomorrow

This Morning

Even the porch swing was a ghost.
Touched perhaps by a light
current of wind sweeping down
from the foothills—
common here in late summer—
but, also as if it was still
telling the story of the night before
trying to find the right words
to finish a last sentence.

He came outside and found himself
there in the little square
of sun splashed on the brick wall
just beyond the swing—
the mess of his hair
the shadow of a familiar monster.

It felt something like a dream—
like he was there
and not there. Like one part of him
had driven out to the coast
the night before—
set out in a solitary dingy
to brave rocking waves and never
made it back.

And another part stayed put
on the porch, spent the entire night
watching the swing sway.

By the time he saw the swing
he'd already decided
waking is like being dead
if the house and other inhabitants
except the cats cooing for food
are still tucked away.

But then a little girl appeared
at the door, her sleepy face pressed
against the glass, her hair
a mess like his, and her mother
behind her (coffee in hand
a ready weapon), eager to deliver
last night's dream.

She'd gone back, she said—
yet again to her grandfather's house.
To carve out the valuables
from the ghosts that own them—
place them gently into living hands.

So, she walked to the garage
and brought back
two rubber alligators—folded
them into lassos—swung wildly
in the air, which whipped.

He understood the desire to perform
such a gesture, rather
than finish any sentence
and wake forever from that dream.

some mornings

I dress in my metaphorical
                               leathers
leash the muse
drag her out
from her slumberous house

throw her on the back of the bike
try to show her a good time

although
most mornings
I commute
to campus

sweating in my synthetic jacket
all terminatored out
to face the battle of the workday

I can't find a line

think of no metaphor
or alliterative phrase

but I don't die   make love
to the pavement
so rough I never rise

I make it home
walk and feed the hound
then myself

it's much simpler
to get away with everything
when getting away
with mere nothing
                            is no cinch

Nightlight

A little moon (mentioned
above) glows in our bathroom—
plugged into a wall socket
below two holes patched with putty
where apparently a towel rack
once hung, which would make three
towel racks in one bathroom.

The single mother and daughter
who lived here before us were okay
with two towel racks, I guess.
But what I really want
to talk about is a magic trail
of rainbow water—a pretend image
I just heard Finn mention
to her mother when I finished using
the bathroom and came out here
to write this down.

But rather than write about
any of that, I sit in a rickety seat
passed down from parents
and listen to night pronounce
its droning arrival in a long drawl
that disappears the light.

I blow smoke through purple petals
drooping on the oxalis our new
neighbors gifted. I flick ashes until
they clump on the webs
North Carolina spider mites weave;
mites hungry enough to gray
every leaf in Greensboro.

At the very least the bush below
the stone ledge that divides
our front porch from the world—
a bush I cannot name. I dare not try.
We just moved here, after all.
I'm still trying to pretend I know
the difference between
the drowning of light and magic
trails of rainbow water.

porch sharks

your lives leap from your lines   spring
from staying put

on a porch   junky
                    littered like a beatnik's
                  all scags & mugs
which would make me
feel at home in greensboro

bc let's face it   we fled

I'll jam the butt
of any inquiry
in an improvised ashtray
maybe a cloudy piece
of tupperware left out for a few days
to feed another likely stray
like it fed me many times before

even vagrants
can stay put too many years

—louisiana-permanence (haha, as if)—
grasping for everything
                      that slithered
                                  further away

than the magic   hand of chance medley

staying put
is a subtle mindfuck
to master
inside the self   outside   ever ever land

there's a shipwrecked son
searching the wake endlessly
for shark teeth singing

Any Poem about Any River

You always damn up
my sharks—

lose them or loose them
in the nearest battleship-shaped
river
        or any poem
          about any river.

I realize now maybe for the first
time maybe the fiftieth
you have always attempted

(somewhere on this map we have
     re-made
       again and again
though cannot name)

to allow me a more pleasant
                        swim—
the exception is always.

Sharing the same map
we have to make a home
in the legend

      because we had to stop
staying put on the porch.

Just today Sarah and I traveled
toward a cat
an hour away in Raleigh
dying of cancer
just to talk options with his doc.

The map app voiced
its list of indiscriminate
                        sentences
at a low volume
on Sarah's phone.

It couldn't get us jack
without catching
every light

        easy as Eric
        before and after
        his dark bout
        with booze.

And to avoid   every toll
we had to listen
to Brett Kavanaugh's opening
statements
        just for
        a distraction.

I wish I could say otherwise
but sometimes
the light holding us is made

        of teeth.

  Sometimes stars
    are sharks   lost

in any river crossed.

sometimes stars are sharks

most times actually—
a ball of burning fangs
they have to move to breathe
twinkle twice razor rows of teeth
swim to grieve
or to bring grief
at the speed of light
really the speed
of death too
if u think as fast as u feel about it
both constants
we urchin behind
with our little human spines
and bottom-feeding
mouths fossilizing doubt
begetting
all these fragile everythings

and sometimes sharks are stars
just as gravity's an aardvark
and mortal tolls
are the only boundaries
for a school of
stellar predators
migrating across sky charts
five dorsal fins
circling dust

II. A PILGRIMAGE TO THE FOUNTAIN OF NOTHING

precarious nothings

I made   a pilgrimage
to the fountain of nothing
wanted to find the source
of all pointlessness
         unsurprisingly
there was no alter of offerings
nor stone engraving
indicating the spring

silent even hidden in grey
foliage or clouds unclear

to me now even before it   still unsure
my response
whether to leap in
splay out my everything
precious   crumbled in a paper sack
or possibly to cork it
                       but my martyr drive
has never been a particularly
strong one   always an acorn
on concrete next to the vivid
spectrum of my hedonism

         which I admit may be shrinking

whether from a slight change
of perspective connected to perseverance
or just the nature of the pendulum

even at this precipice
of the sublime void   even eating a popsicle
favored or flavored by existentialists
there's certainly no spot
for a hammock and my bladder
                              is full
                                of sierra nevada

I open a book
ferlinghetti
and I dance swaying   like a drunk
on the subway
refusing to touch the handrails

                        and consume
the pages madly flipping
to the next to the next
vaulting from word to word
an acupuncture
of mind and body
as if the book
unlike this
seemingly innocuous

wellspring   will never end

Lately

I often wonder if we live
in one of five or six
postcards Brett has sent since
we moved from New Orleans.

I wonder if that kind of living is
the same as inhabiting
windows walked by on the way
to the bodega, say

the one I used to walk to
almost daily for beer or butter.
Maybe an onion or avocado.

In Greensboro we walk
to the park two blocks. Pause
on the little bridge over
the little creek to watch or feed
the little ducks.

When we're hungry we drive
to the closest store we can find.

New Orleans to here I can't
imagine all the bridges
crossed or the rivers their long
frowns stretch always over.

Every one of them is still stuck
somewhere. Wild as a dream
in the Nissan's rearview mirror.
We had to sell that car.

Now, here, we live in wonder
of what we left behind
and what we wait to come
in the mail or otherwise the sky.

air mail

why do we always lie
about the sky
heavenly heavens to betsy
stealth bombers
drones, storks
9/11, santa claus
chemtrails, aliens
earhart, jesus
icarus, wright
lord of the call button
firsts in fastening

I think of paper planes
dreamcatchers
wind chimes
whooping cranes
a flock of kamikazes
hear flight of the valkyries
when pigs have flown
to protect us
they have that right
pilots are actually really smart
some of my boyhood's
favorite heroes
(replaced by joysticks)
many a young american
idolizes—breast pinned with wings—

still my favorite
of the people
that follow orders
and drop disorder

I always wanted to
start a company of
dishwasher safe sex toys
and attachments
and use the profits
to bomb fundamentalist
countries christian and muslim
with said sex toys
so I guess I'm a terrorist
or maybe just another dreamer
with the reflection of horizon on my visor
mach 3 at altitude

it's how we fast forward
from history
in escape pods
pushing the envelope
licking
our love letters to the past

      out there in the ether
the only color to be seen
earthly blues—

a dim faded denim
delivering a fleshy peek
of cheek walked past
with wink caught you
looking back in space

getaway cars

    i.

I can only remember
half of what I remember
    every getaway chase

(who was your girl in *the chase*
again?)

sometimes it was a simple walk
away like at the mall stealing
cards, cds, or video games

sometimes a running vw bus
in idaho after nabbing hubcaps
or high hats for my new best friend

sometimes running through moonlit
fields in the bush
machine guns
and dogs in the near distance

one blast mistakable for a car backfiring
is never as scary as rapid fire
whisper-opera zipping past

once at 14   I went to the projects
to buy forty dollars of weed
with my friend billy
who could drive
that was my first 9mm to the head
I mostly remember the red synthetic interior
of billy's pontiac, the depth down the barrel
eye-to-chamber and our tutor
of hard knock's protruding bottom lip
like a hippopotamus on the nature channel
luckily we were oxpeckers   parasites
allowed to live inside   his lips
ajar so I went home and cut the lawn
sculpting the only grass I got that day
into undulating patterns bloodlessly
self-propelling away thanking god in shock

the first time I walked into an american dispensary
I thought *this was the way it was always meant to be*
always could have been
simple like a candy store
not even as forlorn as an alcohol run

but then how would you ever harm
how would you ever earn   or enslave?

bc every getaway leads to another getaway
I've got more than I've got fingers and toes
I've got some un-getaways too

some nights in the drunk tank
some nights in worse

it's the everything really
that I remember   the whole
feeling of mortal wonder
one either forgets or strives to—
a luna moth that resumes
after its eyed wings are pawed
by human hand after hand
bc my illicit activities pale
in comparison to the number of times
I've avoided dying in a car or plane
or climbing cliffs
by the sea in darkness

even the many times
I entertained finally not letting myself get away
any longer
it all inspires a little fear
(like watching my very own failed murderer of myself movie)

now my conscious mind gravitates to longevity
but even then I honestly can't say I still don't cull that feeling
bc there's nothing more freeing
than being alone   opening up the throttle
on my motorcycle until the oncoming white lines become one
with death in the distance   blurring
the world
and getting away—

ii.

a raindrop get away
with everything down
the window pane
gravity more of a "nothing-
gets-away-without"
kinda deal

I just had a dream
that got away from me
like spilled grapes (ain't blue dude)
something about squirting picante
on a meatball sub passing back
and forth eating bites like russian roulette
and I kept dropping my wallet
everywhere I went
there was a feeling of chagrin
after I challenged a native american
to a swim and then I knew I had to collect
the wallet from a dirty pool drain
with a suction urchin of hairs and debris

a lucid dream is always special—
reflexive moment urging
our fuck or flight instincts

let the wild nighttime rodeo
commence with no cowboys
let the bewildering wildebeests roam
be it a traffic jam or stampede of dinosaurs

of course sleep often gets away from me
on the whole
just like its quick-limed memories
    (upon the waking shit I gotta do today)
more evenings than I support
but it's not a sham
it's a kiln for more getaway capers
blue as delft porcelain

    iii.

blame everything
get away with
the width of the margins
we sneak into
or are imprisoned in

waiting for our monopoly man
to bail us out
our phony jabroni
our lotto line homies
the die the free parking
the bail that is my savings account
the atm in orleans parish prison
that's always broken yet
sheriff sends each visitor
in the drunk tank to it
the gray glimmer of an instance of hope
cheapskates on that paper chase

the jerk-off jackpot
the ganjapreneurs
and all their apprentices
the rainy day roll
the oiled dump superfunds
four for foes
for profit prisons

it's all slathered
like shit on a wall
next to your bunk
or your throne
metal or marble
tincture or ton
this con has conned
done been-around
magic slurs
ya heard

bet I know where you got
them shoes—

Chthonic Sheet of Ice

A woman washes
               dishes in
                an underworld.
In another
       she flowers
         her glare.

Shimmers two   glowering eyes
dull against the winter
night beyond   the kitchen window.

There her face is gripped
by its shabby glass.   This

too is an incarceration. Another
was the day she handed my infancy
over to Memphis January—

the coldest winter on record.
That's what she said anyway.

                When memory
of us curled up curled up
inside her like a story that tells
a story about a story.

In one story an image of my mother
washes dish after dish as I sharpen
my eyes behind her back
cutting its shape into   my story

which is as kind as

                    any underworld

          can be. Still—a kind
             of incarceration.

chronic chthonic disorder

I take it on the lam with charon
crypsis on the river styx
loose lips sink   dinghies
lord knows that's always
been my achilles   spiel
gagged with a bribe
this gold holds frost
as well as the darkness   of depths
can't lay lower than the underworld
an old soul in the oldest hole
where telling is the only escape from toiling
prisoners always got something to say
just wait even silent ones out
we all get here the same way
passion and a lack of control
a lengthy stroll downriver
searching for what we lost
past the past   past the marsh
swallowing each step
with more muddy hunger
our crab traps are broken
so you pull up the neighbors'
when they're not looking
who wants the claws
when you can eat the tails in hell
it's the smell really that brings me back
and the hordes of people filing   filling
their flesh with voids   last pleasures

more a sight for sucking everything in
than even a fish market
or a race track
more viral than alive
a katabasis clap back
the most gruesome of getaways
it's a wish awash
a virtual burial rite
for those that don't ever want to see
past the night

Past the Night

The broken basketball goal
ditched out back by the last tenants
lends its rust to the chain-link fence
it leans against, which divides
our backyard from the neighbors—
four college kids who party
late every Tuesday and Thursday
as if penciled in on a schedule
that's taped below the bar
at the local dive down the street
where they all seem to work.

It's hard to stay angry with them.
We were wild like them and not
that long ago, but we moved to this
neighborhood, with its three-
story UNCG professor homes, its
fancy park, thinking surely
the kids were drinking elsewhere.

We like to drink, too, but usually
on the front porch—what
we're used to after having lived
so long in New Orleans, where only
the rich or lucky have backyards
big enough to sit around and sip.

Sitting on the front porch, the sound
of our aging shame can't travel
downhill straight through a baby's
bedroom window. And we can't play
ping-pong like the kids next door
because we don't have a table or
loud friends. We left them behind
stuck in an old song.

We have this rusted basketball goal
which is silent except the sound
of dead leaves scratching through
the pink hoop and behind
the backboard. We score every lie
we tell ourselves about its past
every time we see it lay in its waste.

I guess it's hard to curb something
like a broken basketball goal
when you move out. It's not a couch
which we curbed on Joliet and again
on Gayoso, moving from house
to house when we were priced out
of entire school districts. But
that, too, is a lie—a bit of a *stretcher*
as Mark Twain might've said.

But when we moved to Greensboro
we were told—one of the first
things—everything has to be in a bin.
Won't get picked up otherwise.

So the basketball goal remains
a home for dead leaves or a lookout
for the occasional squirrel
scanning the terrible sky for wings.
And every time I come out
to our new backyard, which is big
for us, to rake up the leaves,
the broken goal is there prompting
me to lie—to say that once
it belonged to a little girl not unlike
our five-year-old daughter Finn,
named after Twain's attempt
to rewrite a false truth—but maybe

this girl was a bit older, and she
got away with everything once upon
a time, but by the time getting away
with everything was already
a story she was beginning to tell
herself, the goal was already
on its side and beginning to brown
like the leaves that pile around it.

The leaves. That's why I'm here—
to rake again. But now I see a quarter
tails up among the elm's dead
which makes me wonder if good luck
belongs to pennies alone.

I rake it into the pile—watch it glint
at the top like an ornament
for a foul cake cooked in hell. But I
feel heavenly enough to quit working—
bend down to put it in my pocket—
return it again to the darkness
it fell from. Maybe later I can magic
a silver dream from Finn's ear.

swallowing spit

man if I had a nickel
for every time I didn't   evade
raking the leaves
a dime for all the times
I've dreamed   to be extinct
a susan b for all the wednesdays
I stayed up all night like your neighbors
man if we still had the quarter (as in vieux carré)...
we'd be sippin coffee   beer   or tea
—no difference to me—on a balcony
showing our faces to the storm
recounting all the getaways we've
aged with minor disgrace, a form of dignity
for former reprobates with silver keg
chests bare except tattoos and hair
with concrete consciences which
the roots of our families wiggle thru and   displace
to form the only topography found
on these streets where the sidewalk bursts
begins ends and begins again every step
a getaway trip   I recall a story
my friend louis running from the cops
and his stinky chef clogs flying off
like rabid bats in the dark
before the block itself easily apprehended   him
what a scene   he was so drunk he went home
to his apartment two apartments ago
pounded furiously on the door screaming for

g-money—another cook and friend as well as
his roommate several roommates ago—to let him in
I washed dishes at a pizza joint on magazine
with a kid with a real similar story
except he let himself into the wrong uptown home
then curled up on the couch
passed out   after the mother shouted and called
the cops to get him out   she felt so bad
she eventually bailed him out
bc he was so broke he had to do a 56-day stint
in opp and this was post-katrina   shortly after
so no telling the things that kid seen   I did 3 days
and cried my eyes out the moment I was released
the most absolute hell I've ever been subjected to
I still remember getting the last sip of backwash from
the one shared cup of water we got over the entire
duration
                                      of course I swallowed it

On the Morning of My 37th Birthday

I spill from a dream   somewhere
between rested   and wrested.

 In which an ancient woman   quivers
  two whispery brooms back
        and forth—
handle-end to bristle-end—
     in the oozy dark until my body
        is gone.

Where its shape had stood   there
is only more night.   The process
is slow.
But my ghost flies   city   to country
so fast I lose track   of how.

Through the bedroom window I hear
shivers of wind rattle dead cans.
                Maybe the rain
hasn't stopped slanting Thursday's sky
into Saturday.
              I check my phone
for the weather—see a familiar
sham sun—   imagine the actual star
glad to be a white dot ensconced
on its shelf   of cloud
ready to rip the morning   apart—
a desperate pink.

Facebook tries to sell me a shirt
Every Capricorn Should Own.
                Its cotton sleeves make long
                  promises
to keep me warm; every stitch
choked—uplifting words about being
born in January;   five different fonts
yawning blue and maroon.

My mother sends a text—all caps.
After her obligatory sentence
three question marks   curl black
inside three black boxes—replacement
for emojis refusing   translation.

I don't mind.   I wonder
why we place   the image
after the word.   I wonder what
balloons   cakes   or confetti?

Yesterday's clothes are wadded
on the floor beside the bed
like a dead animal.   I put myself
through their holes   advance
in a clash   of tremors
toward the kitchen for coffee.

On the table   six blue tulips
Finn picked
for my birthday.   Later

both knowing their scent
is wasted on us non-pollinators
we'll take turns directing our inattention
to the ripe reward   they signal for.

I'll imagine her five-year-old hand
suspended in invisible wind
like a monstrously
misshapen swarm on a long walk
to steal flowers   from the edges
of neighbors' lawns.

Now in the absence of bees   my phone
buzzes in my pocket.   My sister
sends a gif
equipped with lit candle   pointy hat
whiskery cat-face   sassy gray.

I produce a dim smile   for no one—
tantamount to the kitchen's dying bulb;
table the phone next to the laptop;
remember I haven't   spoken
to Vince in two months.
        I've heard
    from his brother
about a girlfriend—   Greek Professor
or   Professor of Greek?
    To hunt down news of her
            I try to read

his last poem   sprawling
so many storied arms like so many
ghostly tentacles.
                              I'm distracted—
because the blur of octopus I saw
a few days ago   with Finn
at the Science Center   focuses
behind my eyes every ten minutes.

It reminds me—then   and now—of what
Vince said once at Chelsea's Bar
                              in Baton Rouge—
that he'd eaten octopus before but
probably wouldn't do it again.   *Hard*
to eat something with so much   heart.

I close the laptop   open
the blinds to have a look before   the sun
cracks
open the morning   spilling
its judgments
hurrying the traffic to work.

On our front lawn   two crape myrtles
wear the dark   like a heavy coat.
The ends of their branches
                              have spread
themselves too thin.
                              I am still here
to sweep the mess of fallen petals;

I am still here to compare   bare branches
to a dream of brooms; I am still here
to write all this down;   I am still
slow in the process
                    of disappearing.

my blur flew from puddle to puddle

I am
still
slow
in
the
process
of
disappearing

some
folks
have
tape
recorders

I have
blur
and
a ship's
memory

a
more
reliable
fallible

a
rebel

with
so
much
heart

see
I
don't
recall
the
site

just
the ritual

nor
the
sentence

just
the
sentiment

all
toxin
confetti
absurd
trivia
of my
specter

three
blue
hearts
of
an
octopus

sure
maybe
I want
more
nothings

an
ink
cannibal

but
I made
friends

currents
lifting
me
from
trench
to
trench

my ghost flew from city to country

yesterday it was so foggy
walking home from the library
I couldn't see the new church's tower
just the smaller two twin steeples
and there was a confidence in knowing
there's something so large looming invisibly
the cathedral's ghost I believed in more than
any greater significance of church
I have yet to climb that tower
unseen and filling this traveler
with an irregular flight of faith
on this particular evening pass
too windy every time I've tried
and even though you can't smell them
anymore or visit the crypt
you can read an eyeful inside
about how the hollows
are packed with royal bones
delft—a painter's town
of two church towers
one old and one new
and the resting place until this day
—or opaque evening to be precise—
for the house of orange
where the assassination of william
by a fanatic catholic was the first
assassination with a handgun
in history combined with the fact

the spanish had sacked breda
predecessor home of royal bones
so here he stayed
away from greater cities
hosting greater ghosts
and I think about my own
little disappearing act
from everything
how the fog welcomes
only what is in front of it
a lesson particularly
useful for apparitions

sweeping et al.

under the proverbial table
my leather pants

—the ones from spain
I'd lost my virginity in—

got away
from me in the 11th grade
my buddy pete
that sonofabitch

—who just like a rich kid
never offered to pay—

borrowed them for prom
and I never saw them again

—not without implication
I did take off on a pink camel
bloody his nose with my knee
doing a deer spirits-fueled antler dive
off a pool chair he held

actually I loved his mom very much
and not just because she bought
some knives from me
the summer I pretended to work
before my first break for paris

often I'd stroll into her house
—in idaho no one knocks or locks—
to converse with her just
as often as I'd go to see pete
essentially we lived
on the same street
she was always happy
to see me—

which was rare for parents
in those days especially

she'd greet me loudly
exuding a sanguine glow
and her whole-noted hoot
that sounded like a sailor
who'd just heard a doozy
followed up with a slightly
more feminine snicker
then she'd resume raking her carpet

—can of oil in the periphery that
paced her throughout her chores—

ever-inquiring about the how of me
and, not explicitly, craving a tinge
of the trouble I was up to
as she'd go back and forth
we'd go back and forth
like stuck buddies do

my favorite is when I'd find
her in the chilly garage
next to pete's dad's harley
and the fridge full of aluminum
she never offered me

—she probably knew
I was usually a little lit too
escaping
the commandments
of my parents—

she'd reminisce
about her annual rides
to sturgis
sure you could hear
her giddy even over
a hog's resounding
combustion
of the getaway fantasy
companionship
so often needed when sharing
a broom

chess pieces untidily scattered

one rarely liberates themselves from the burdens of birth
the temerity of family
the boredom and belligerence we show
who we love most
we police most
pull tails   make squeal
like torturing daddy long legs
or stuffing m80s in frogs
the cruelty and ignorance
we are capable of before we are fully molded
into a tundra of persona
which the gods taught us
and a consolidated god robbed us
of our piece of the crab apple pie
out of the trivial pursuit of passions
our colonoscopy of ontology
old poisons grow evermore poisonous
and the contagions of connection
or correction bestowed upon us brethren
resist the timorous
swallow the backwash
all tainted pail and well
our flashback backfired
before all stumbling aftermath—
howbeit don't lie down your king just yet

okay, boomer

watching all the old boomers get away
with doing nothing at all their meetings
the audible and edible consternation
of the faculty of the administration
of the people getting everything
we usually just want to get away from
yet to many I have become one
maybe even to myself
society is sick of watching the elite and their getaways
all except one so maybe they aren't as sick
as me bc their man is nothing but a finger
up their butt with some arsenic on top
the grocery list scrolls down endlessly
all my outsider sentiment conflicts with
all my hetero cis whiteness
and the unanswered abjections
society wages against realer others
than myself are loftier than any thought
yet all our promises to ourselves
more often than not are
the things we have no choice
is it wrong to derive some joy
splitting the see-you-in-hells
is it wrong for moses to rejoice
between conjoined tidal waves
overhead their break impending

III. CHURN THE EARTH

Jack's Ashes

    I.

We keep them cached
in a box. Its shade
of brown often only a color
faux wood can claim.
Its size and shape
tantamount to discounted
soap, two bars packed
and sold together—
about as heavy as that.

The entertainment center
it sits on was passed
down from my grandfather
when I was seven—
a long time before he died
and a much longer time
before I met Sarah,
my wife, and Jack, her cat.

Jack was Siamese—at least
part. The black M
crested on his forehead
suggested something else—
Maine Coon maybe—
but we never really knew.

As for the heirloom,
Grandpa said cherry wood.

Who can really tell
what anything is made of
if it wanders in on all fours—
abandoned warehouse
to abandoned world—
or is handed down
from a failure of memory
to tell history's lies
until it finds a new wall
to rest against.

The entertainment center—
its awkward wobbly
frame—weighs the same
as 500 boxes of ashes.
All the size of discounted
soap—two bars packed
and sold together;
this is one lie I could tell.

And if I was asked to tell
how many times
I've hauled it from house
to house, I think
I'd describe the dying
legs it stands on instead
but only as things

that grow closer to claws
with every move.

II.

I remember wanting
to help haul Grandpa's box
to its muddy hole.
I remember it felt wrong
the job was given
to his brothers alone.

I had to stand by watching
the rain churn the earth.

III.

I'd thought Sarah wanted
to scatter Jack's ashes
but she must've decided
against it, because there's
no way to open the box.

It was Sarah who Googled
Greensboro pet burial.
She went with *Precious
Memories*—the sixth hit just
below *Dead Animal Pickup*.

IV.

My grandfather's body
never would've been
burned to ash. It's just not
what my family does.
We're delivered
to the dirt cold and whole—
too stiff to change
the shape of death for us
still standing graveside
holding our breath.

When we die we're stilled
by the absence of will.
Gone too soon
to stop pretending
we live forever—
never a grave slip
of signed paper to get
to the desk. There is little
to leave either way.

V.

Jack left us a shadow
slinking along baseboards—
memory striped with fur

his long body blinked
easily away.

Grandpa left little behind
save the gravelly sound
of his voice caught on a VHS—
a family video of his 25th
wedding anniversary.

It's hard now to recall
the words those sounds
propped up, but I like
to remind myself that
the tape still exists
somewhere—it must.

    VI.

We said Jack was part
Maine Coon. It wasn't
necessarily a lie.
Saying so just made life
a lighter defeat.
Grandpa said cherry wood
when he passed on
the entertainment center
like a shot in a movie
most overlook.

VII.

The entertainment center—
it has no measurable mass.
We know
only how heavy it feels
when we move from house
to house, when we hold it
close to our chests, when we
peel it from the floor
where its claws gripped.

VIII.

Jack never woke up
and our other cat started
peeing all over the floor.
Maybe she had been before.
Maybe it was the move.
Maybe it was because she knew
Jack was dying before her.

She's better now, but now
we might move again.
Sarah says she's applying
to a new opening
at a school three hours
into the mountains.
I imagine the scratches

that will be left on the floor
from those legs
clawing their initials
into the wood.

      IX.

This morning I remain
unimaginative
concerning the question
of everything—
of whether or not
to be burned or buried
or whether it's better
to say *grandpa* or
grandfather

              —all I know

is to hear his voice
we have to stay asleep.

alt burial rites

I too have been envious
of pallbearers
            excluded
(probably for my youth
or smaller stature)
from the last time
you have to help
someone make
a move

we two have been
brothers in dirt
waterlogging
our dreams
to make them even
heavier

chasing them
or the cat
or the tail
often our own

to bury
our dead
the bones
or barbeque
them into
the biblical dust
we were promised

decisions
w/o revisions

black holes
swallowing
white holes

no funerals
or wills
and infinite funerals
and wills

in spacetime

we get the distance
to solve everything

unable to reach our
alternate selves

we will long
for the burdens
of this shadow
world we wait
to be burned into

gonna set your flag on fire

big chef been calling me about wild man again
(one must wonder how many conversations
like this have gone on behind their back)
how he's become unhinged
disappearing and reappearing   wasted   missing work
threatening to murder movie producers
and his former partner   best friend
enough to be the only one still talking
about an intervention
and what kind of friend or flag boy
am I when I talk him out of it
say that our wild man's
too far gone   living on stolen time
which is the greater crime
to care or not care
to let or try to stop him
maybe call his dad or mental health?
(even if it's not for me now   I do believe
it's everyone's right to kill themselves
I'm sure people have accused me of the chore)
shit someone else probably
called the cops already
the big chef's text read "jail or coffin"
and everyone that knows wild man
knows there are guns and a sports car
idling near   not to mention
camels coke beer weed shrooms xtc
lsd poppers speed and maybe meth

in whatever shape form or quantity
they make it these days   me being
not as initiated in such things anymore
besides the occasional concert
camping trip   excuseless debauchery   or mardi gras
(and hey I've got no problem
with drugs   myself or in society
even though people I love
have probably felt quite the opposite)
this caring requires careful planning
like a getaway   some tricky shit
it's so much more fun easy and desperate
to not give a fuck and that's where our wild man's at
and I been there believe me   but he's settled there
—maybe longer than anyone I know—
to the point of martyrdom
and wasn't judas the best disciple?
someone will believe jesus was a burner and lived in the quarter
he certainly loved the prostitutes altho now he has the scene
and fuck I do get a kick running into the kid
(I won't lie sometimes he provides and I take)
at cosimo's or the track and he's shaking his skinny ass
snapping vivid photos   passing a good time
cracking us up shit faded ashy and falling out as he may be
we've got real history and I love the joker even if I
yearn for a former version   one I really identified with
(a fellow car-wreck orphan   I respected his hustle and ambition
shit did this already get in the past tense?)
even so I don't entirely fault him for his decisions
(he's certainly evolved out of his southern prejudices)

it's a fucked up world and he's making it fun   fucking it back
I get that—fuck I do the same—even though I haven't let go
to the same degree   in fact my grip has tightened
but does that mean I'm more or less enlightened?
it certainly doesn't feel right when you let a friend get away
even if it's to a body-painted paradise of vice
don't see his dealers or burner family
coming up with bail or a shot
of adrenaline when he needs it most
because there's no extricating him from them or new orleans
nor can we longer enjoy the spectacle of friend-killing
so we guiltily choose distance and our own cold getaway
from a friend so long in need that it becomes greedy
neither of us are gonna bail him out next time
and none of us want to go to his funeral
I'm sure I've told him as much in between beers
maybe keybumps before bed
but this violence is what poisons our aid
running around with guns and threatening
that's where I gotta stay on the neutral ground
I've spent my time with nopd and la doc
in truth I'm trying to leave the whole damn country
not a felon and soon   so here you go wild man:
not even this poem can be your intervention
and I never felt like I was ever in a place myself to give one
considering I'll probably party next to you this very weekend
but to you my friend deep below the shell of sequins
and chemicals   from one brokenhearted motherless brother
to the other I say: please   please prove this poem wrong

Too Dark to Tell

The sky is full
of black and screaming

—Bill Callahan, "Too Many Birds"

Just before my mother called
to deliver the difficult news
that my brother attempted to take
                                   his own life
           I snapped a pic
of the biggest owl I've seen so far

                  in North Carolina.

Its shadowy bulk flew from rooftop
to crape myrtle
and I saw the lawn for the first time
                         with wild eyes.

The feathery predator perched—
its pinions folded on a bare branch—
           prepared to take
the life of the stray calico
       slinking below.

Not quite kitten and not quite cat
it was one of those that always looks
adolescent.

      I hadn't seen it before;
      the owl must've.

My mother called twice
           knowing the first will go
straight to voicemail
              the second will ring.

It didn't take long
        for us both to stop talking—
        unable to unknot.

Where rope ends and sky begins
was too dark to tell.
              I hung up—

deleted the pic—too dark to tell

    owl from tree.

Measurements

The sun too is given a size—numbers
for height and width?
                         I don't know if that's right.

Though replace both with
a Shakespearean—or gothic—phrase
as in   *from crown to toe*
and you'll approximate me   could if you cared
to look long enough.

See   here I am   feet stretched out
back hunched
on porch steps
hiding the odd from the even   even

        from my neighbor   who always
is smoking on her front porch   always
on her phone.

Just across the thicket   where the rabbits
have made their warren   between
the shadows of our homes   darkening
the grass

she sits where she has sat   since the day
she lost her job.

Today I stayed home   took the day off.

A mental health day I told my boss and
the woman who haunts this house   with me

the woman who opened the curtains
like she does   to let in some sun

like she does
before she left   dropped our daughter off
at school.

Two degrees earned and I   haven't learned
much because
even from this   distance
        (also somehow
          measurable)

we can attach numbers to define the diameter
                               of the sun
           and I can't even tell
the woman who haunts the house
after she's gone

(crumpled bedsheet discarded beside me dead)

to show the bright world her
painted face

        how cowardly I become only an hour
        after it rises—

won't mention a thing about the blades
sharpening themselves inside my fattening
belly
or
the constant throb in my chest   that I
want it all to quit.

Still I sit holding smoke in my mouth—
still I won't stop sitting   so long so often
on the porch
              hiding from my neighbor

myself
and the sun.

Like one of those scared rabbits   its chest
thumping 150 beats per minute

I only come out of hiding
              an hour before dark

the curtains not yet closed
              but promised.

IV. THIS NEVER-ENDING THEATER

everything possible

last night a young man my age
pleasant yellow hair and a pale face
came to me at my work with curious pictures
of us together   yet apart   from distanced childhood
altho he wouldn't introduce himself or state his claim
he promised all would be revealed when he came back again
my father was there too and took no notice
this stranger visited and left again with equal dubiousness and aplomb
yet I confronted my father   forced him to assure me I had no estranged
brother from secret infidelities   a bastard to haunt us
in the third eye of evening he came again   this time with a homemade
show-n-tell that in sentiment would have   made cornell proud
a handheld sculpture of toothpicks my mother used
a fly collection from our small apple orchard in ny
little illegible scribbles all over   triggering suspicion in me
(why a writer suspects the writing...)
a saran-wrapped yellow mangled shoebox of liquid and a few wires
a digital trigger he fumbles out of his pocket
not quick enough to curtail the assault I level on him
and fail to restrain to the point of pulping his head
albeit in a cartoon not gory way since everything is possible
in this poem

groping for consent

in the late 80s
even early 90s
sex education
had pbs and pamphlets
at the dept of health
and pornography
was found in the woods
sold in black sleeves
seedy street clubs
hwy stops
or doled out in fractions
over dial up
the concern on the tip
of every tongue
and titillation was hiv
a shared fear by gays
blacks   whites
(never any presidents)
prostitutes   even virgins
like me and all the other kids
that watched the movie *kids*
back then the word consent
wasn't discussed
with much hierarchy
in the lexicon
one could presume
it was assumed
boys should be gentleman

when making out
and groping
for permission
to satisfy
instincts
to go as far
as persuasion
and a girl would let you
certainly stop
when you heard
the word no
but that was consent
either an implication
or a steadfast strikeout
and to be even
more up front
what adolescent
boy amidst
heavy petting
and getting handsy
as they used to say
isn't flooring it
to get to his primitive
goal of the promised
land to *lie* with a woman
another   problem
language exposes
consent's not promised
(except by myths of every hollywood
rom com, tv show, not to mention

a pervasive promise of all advertising)
but bestowed
and the folks in palo alto have yet
to write a great regression
for applying brakes
in the heat of the moment
and why would they?
because sex is capital
but now   and rightfully so
consent is a larger fraction
of the dialogue
that's something
to be proud of
yet the predator president
flaunts how he evades a cage
and professors and poets
cave to trigger warnings
outrage and self-censorship

Normal Stranger Ogling Octopus

I hear the prerecorded message
reach through a speaker hidden somewhere
in the ceiling above gate B-45
warning in a white-woman-radio voice
not to accept foreign objects from strangers.

I consider reaching toward the woman
to my left—to the tattooed octopus reaching
red tentacles down the side of her thigh.

> To offer the book
> I'm about to finish.

I tell myself it would be funny to do that.
Tats, nose ring, shaved sides of scalp—
all must mean she's someone
who finds that kind of foolishness
just a little funny.

> Instead I check
> the time again.

Maybe she isn't scared of the sudden
death of reading, and doesn't need any help
holding a laugh in the unmoving air.
Likely she *is* scared of any normal stranger
reaching an unprompted hand her way.

On the plane, she sits in front of me, texting
a loved one left behind or one
she's on her way to see.

    I look away
    to prove I'm good.

negative capability

hemingway's heroes I am not
a bridge dynamiter
in *for whom the bell tolls*
fighting fascists
for my father
but there's some killer
deep in my dreams
sometimes he succeeds
in his war against me
sometimes I violate
and reap revenge
over
and over   on him
we are both   victims
and perpetrators
returning

two enemas down /
one to go

living involves an everything or two
I would have rather avoided
the first one directed at my navel
my clenched ass rejected
more of a rim wash than
how it was supposed to go
sheets covered in saline
and me stretched and confused
but not runnin to the bathroom
got the trick of it the second time
finally accepting my fate
and mainly from the fear
of not complying with orders
these methods
were called for
by the colon and rectal specialist
an attractive female one at that
kept me talkin about that time I got the bends
while she did a lil cave dive of her own
(she prob logged quite a few that day)
ascending she informed me I have a fistula
or in layman's terms:
a tunnel in my ass
(the poetic implications of that are so vast
they are almost boring)
which led to this present predicament
evacuating and writhing in pain

on the only throne this world's giving me
but in preparing for a tiny surgery
I figure if I'm getting everything out
might as well get out a poem

anesthesia if you please
gimme the adult cuff
on the bed rail
the taped body hair
the curtains adorned
with cursive vines
blossoms orange
and ugly as
my broken ass
the ceiling chirping fluorescent
almost overtakes the acoustic
elevator music banality not
the neighbor's diagnosis
with a side of tears
a spoon-fed joke
the dose of laughter
sticking it to yourself
before the unknown
an investment in health
after a year of being bullied
by the body

Here Comes the Rain

Between the sea and the salt marsh
my in-laws' bijou beach house squats on stilts
above a thicket of cordgrass
and bluestem, where for the last two nights
some critter, hidden from my phone's
dim flashlight in the brush below the back deck
has made its noise toward the water.

It's Mother's Day. Sarah's mom sits
on the deck, reading while she reclines
in a plastic Adirondack; Sarah, silent beside her,
does the same—a book on women surrealists
held up awkwardly to block the sun.

The kid's couched, gripped by the unflinching eye
of an iPad, so I step out to ask the mothers
if they'd prefer that I go to the closest grocery
for cinnamon and vanilla—I'd promised
to cook French toast. *Appetite doesn't demand it*
Sarah says. Her mother's nod agrees.

I point out a kettle of hawks sporting the blue
above a lone cormorant—the span
of its unfolded wings meant to intimidate
any predators. Sarah nudges past me
to grab the binoculars that belong to the house.

When she's finished she passes them to me
and returns to the tabled book. I fumble to adjust
the settings, scan the scar of land
jutting out from the marsh but can't spot
the cormorant. Instead I find the American flag
at the edge of the neighbor's deck.

Last night, after everyone had gone to bed
a strange shadow whipped
back and forth across the marsh. I didn't know
right away what the black swath
belonged to, but when I attached shadow
to flag, I wished I had the drugs needed
to help me see it—to face or forget whatever it
might've meant. I mention this to Sarah—
make my noise toward the kitchen.

At the oven I'm still holding the binoculars.
Dizzy from looking through their lenses
I stumble back to the deck—hand them over.
But before I head in I notice the sky
blurring a bit, swearing an oath to rainclouds
and remember that roar
we'd heard at the beach the last two days—
like the sky was shedding its skin.

We thought at first it had to be planes hidden
by clouds; a rumble of thunder.
But there were no clouds at all. I thought

of what Jack Kerouac said about the sea, which
I read on the little square of embroidery
decorating the toilet in the guest bathroom.
That it must be *the roar of eternity.*

I think now there must be a major insinuation
I'm missing—now, the moment
when the rain begins to come down.

roaring an oath to rainclouds

my binocs
broke   before jack

like when we all fell outta love with neal
after he dosed us the last time

we thought our lovers
were capable of   embroidering eternity

finding surrealists in the sun
solving a generous family feud in the sand

or making   our making

princely pancake
without vanilla   or cinnamon

neighbors
without freighters

feathers   without a flag

       we weld the tunnel
         while the gods sleep

all we need   is to need it all

grand slam

there are as many
ziploc bags
as there are suns

I'll go breaking anything
yes after a homerun
still steal second base

we sandbag our meat
rests to bleed

go ahead
enjoy being led to the drought
throw your arms
in the trickle of river tonight

go ahead
velcro our lips together
kindling the vows
of a bonfire

nothing
can take us over
not even infinity's
only moment

missing booth inside your head

when time is ringing in my ears
I pick up

you & sarah calling
from the national show

held shitty mic up
to speaker like the 90s

I couldn't make
song thru all the satellite

but the blips and yelps
were all poetry and party

I suspect it may have been
"I'm afraid of everyone"

I've ever used
which is everyone

including you two
two of my besties

imagining you both
on a date in dc

makes me pleased
as the greek professor

not professor of greek
makes me a feast

consisting of so much feta
oil, olives, and oregano

sex &
tzatziki
the real viagra
besides weed & wine

how many summer moves
have we moved and moved on

how we make a home
how we make love

in our cells
across our phones

the clichéd poem in a bottle (personally emptied)
cast into the brainy briny seas

if we stay anywhere trouble will find us (inevitably)
if we'd stayed there (nola) we'd never leave

but in order—even if chances were entropy—to get away
one must get away with (nothing and) everything

In the Wake of Chthonic Fires

The fragile chimera of a child's laugh
skips across the hardwood, from living room
to kitchen—aging secondhand sofa
to dirty dishes—breaking a bit as it goes.

The broken parts roll to the corner baseboards
where they collect in piles pretending to be old dolls
tossed aside, stray markers with lost tops,
moments of time when it was somewhat harder
for laughing to happen. The part of the laugh

that remains intact, having refused an afterlife
that silence demands, makes its way to the woman
washing dishes, in which a creature is always
cresting the dark caves of her blood, as if
each morning the sun mounts the blue belly of sky

the coldest night is gone for the first time—this
is one part of her that is named Mother;
the part that hears the sound of laughing over water
that woos hands to hurry; over hip podcast voices
battling for a second to say something funny;

or a newscaster tongue, which moves like a monster
not because of how loud it speaks, or the tone—
because of the words it shapes. The mother,
alone, hears the child's laugh like a sentence said
in a dream after waking—impossibly.

And she won't be stirred by disbelief. Just today
her daughter asked if her face could be
painted like a rainbow-cat; surely we all know
the laugh that follows is a tangible fantasy.

lost tops

we've followed tangible fantasies
for at least an eternity
intangible ones
for how long?

I don't write fuckin algorithms

I throw my soul
on the floor
to be kicked
around like
marker tops
all cylindrical
and hollow
all yellow
and roll

I'll take the finger
my many   venial
         misdemeanors
but whose lord
gets charged for the felonies?

supposing
it's only omni-hardnosing
I'm syphoning

exceptional fire:
water up the nose
that involuntary tingle
(just like fire and language)
is a gift from the gods
(lest we forget
even our captors
have captors)

Said the Night at Intermission

          It's one of those days I never had
before the move.

I pour a cheap beer in a fancy glass
wait at the antique table falling apart

                                in the kitchen
while Sarah finishes Finn's
bedtime routine.

My ritual of reading having ended
as it does   with a kiss
                I sit and try to recall

the name of the tropical bird
painted in fiery streaks across
my fancy glass but never can.

In the oppressive   electric light of a kitchen
at night
       I elicit instead
                      a specific sashay
                      of memory.
Not recollected
as if from a past life regression.

More alive and well than that—more
                              breathing
                        now than then.

As if the night itself has drilled into my skull—
an intermission
to make room—to glorify its own
not-so-gruesome operation. And this memory

springs dancing   from the burr hole
like so:

There is a strange woman   in the kitchen.

She creeps like wild wallpaper   or a flicker
of sun against its flowers   when a window
of trees invites it in.

Floorboards creak beneath her boots
as a stage for her sort of performance would.

In a moment I'll flick a flake
of crusted skin from her forehead.

She'll frown.   For now she's happy

to stop changing clothes every five minutes
to walk a goofy walk.

And she won't stop—she can't until I believe
in its beauty. It's easy to get
distracted from couch and book   if you are

an audience of one.

I give her the typical green-light giggle
we both need to hip-pivot past
our own darkening eruptions—then she's off

        to find the perfect sweater-
            skirt combo.

In a moment   she'll be gone
to meet a friend—
    to booze through afternoon.

Sitting by the window   at Molly's Irish Pub
       she'll become something
    the sun shimmies by.

For now she's happy to be a strange woman
creeping over the kitchen's creaky boards

as beautiful as wild as strange as light
as flower as paper   as I am grateful.

    —And look now here she comes.

I pour a fancy beer in a cheap glass

always been one
for sacrament
over ceremony

(ceremony
over sacrifice?)

of coffee mugs
over designer drugs

of moving through
the house party
to the kitchen

and reaching into a new
patchwork cupboard
that awaits my selection of evening

the first morning I listened
with my eyes I heard the screaming
of a spider on her web

suctioned by the wind
like this glass I'm holding
blown by machines

making minimum wage
in mother russia
sold by ikea

full of all the OW
—a cherry sour
found in a den in delft
boasting 700 beers—
I could afford

as much as anyone feels
—the slick bourgeois cup they grasp in—
this unnecessary world is theirs

as much as I prefer the next morning
surprise
after being up all night yard sale find

V. UNDESERVING OF FURTHER RESOLVE

Family Reunion at the Hunting Lodge

On Father's Day, one father—
among many—is granted an hour
or two to hide under a tree;
jot down his thoughts.

The bugs are too bad—or too many
maybe—for him to stand
the fuss of their unrelenting whispers;
the occasional pang
of exposed ankle or calf.

And his few lines are likely to be
either impossibly pastoral
or undeserving of further resolve.

But he decides he'd like to try anyway;
grabs his daughter's clipboard—
her new set of glittery pens
and slick paper from the patio table
scattered with spent cans
and abandoned bottles of water.

He creaks open the cooler and pockets
two beers; drags his father-in-law's
red camping chair—
the one with two cup holders—
to the closest shade tree
far enough away from the family.

Alone, he spends the next half hour slapping himself in the face.

Snaggletooth

I'm already questioning whether or not
I can get away with using that word—
if I can say *snaggletooth* and be taken seriously.
But that's what Sarah said when she got back
to Greensboro from her new position
an hour out of town. *Look at my snaggletooth*
she said—*broke biting my thumbnail.*

Surely, I should mention a few key facts
if I want *snaggletooth* to sail. It was her first day
on the job, for example, and her nerves
were something like a shipwreck after our move
from New Orleans. No one could blame her
for taking any action against anxiety she had
at her fingertips—as the day's images
danced past—as the pines lining the highway
scrolled across the window or her Yaris.

I'll just go ahead and say *central incisors*
to establish that her front teeth (the upper two)
have both been fake since sixth grade.
Her dentist decided that she must've swum
underwater—her thin lips parted—so often
the chlorine nearly gnawed the enamel to pulp.
There's really no other way to explain it
Sarah remembers the man saying.

Now I wonder if I should lie—say that Sarah
was driving to work rather than home—
to invite you to see her stand behind a podium.
Look, stage-right, most of her central incisor
is missing—new students' terrible eyes gawking.
Sarah keeps forgetting to stop parting
her lips, when, every few seconds, she smiles.

But now it looks like I can't avoid the truth.
Now when Sarah glides across the room
to find me at the table's dark corner. And after
she leans over for a kiss, asks about my dreams
like she does—her warm breath heavy
with sleep—she skims that last bit about the lie.
Promptly informs me that, actually, she had been
on her way to work, then suggests I add in
a few key facts I hadn't planned on providing.

Instead of getting too into that now, I wonder
if I can fit in the dream I had last night—
a dream Sarah didn't ask about, because I made
that part up. She does ask me often
about my dreams, but she didn't this morning
and this morning I woke from a dream
in which I shit my pants. Even stumbled through
the dark hall to the bathroom—wiped my ass.

It was the first time I'd ever had that dream.
I remember nothing else. And when
I wiped my ass there was nothing there. I guess
that's all I'll say about it, which likely means
I don't need to bring it up at all, that I should
probably focus on Sarah's snaggletooth.
But it looks like I'm failing—or is it *flailing*?

So maybe I'll start to wrap this up, tell you that
once the tooth was replaced with a new
porcelain temporary, Sarah broke it biting—
central incisors first—into an apple a week later.
And she happened to be on the way home
to Greensboro from her new position an hour
out of town. But at this point, if you're still
listening, how can you believe anything I say?

If you believe I ever wanted you to believe
I was always telling the truth—yes, I have failed
or one of us has. I just wanted to invite you
to see Sarah holding her broken tooth
as she drove home, to see it resting on the bed
of an awkward palm, so she wouldn't lose it.
I wanted you to see her saunter in minus a tooth.
And, if you haven't yet, to see her lips part
to make room for her smile—then

just after—to hear her say *snaggletooth*. To feel
something like gratitude when I tell you now
she eats with the corner of her mouth—
careful not to be too hungry to forget. But really
sometimes I just need to let someone know
how she makes me flail, which feels
something like smiling underwater, a mouthful
of pool held at the ready to squirt between
my teeth—still smiling—when I come up for air.

to turn the other cheek

the good book says
much dreaming
and many words
are meaningless
which seems
a biased proclamation
for a deity
and scripture
that both start
with words
but also one a poet
or fellow misfit
can swallow
easier than
the best getaway
caper of all time:
resurrection

how much hubris
we have to have
to say no thanks
to the rest of the words:
therefore fear god
and turnaround
and believe in words
            in dreams

even earth
now known as nature
still spinning at this present
moment with no suspected
getaway without some kind of faith
dreams come on judgment eve

disinvited to the soulless sugar-coated banality of the average family day outing

whether one begins or ends w/ amen
doesn't qualify them as my friend
not sure really what does
besides the years of
not forgetting or
forgetting
the getting
or not getting
away
(or just being there)
with everything
or nothing
maybe the roar
of vulnerability
heard from a recess
definitely delinquency
buzzed from an excess
served in the wrong goblet
graffiti'd putrid pewter
bone-in ambrosia
listening to morning dew
well past an apocalyptic
'72 afternoon spooned
well into the future
without friends or you
without everything
or nothing

lurking in the glow

—*for angeliki*

one part dust
one part mud
fill with shadow
flood
with lust
for stolen flesh
and language
grow into a powerful thirst
a gloomy gluttony
no more or less holier
than thou
than the horizon
the seam of night
earth's largest shadow
suffocates starlight
from reaching
the monstered ocean
in our scavenging hearts
fare forward
with little choice
besides the getaway
drop   atop
a halo
so when you find
that rare
angel in space
self-jettison into
her radiance
lurk in her glow

drive thru confessional, unframed

sure I've gotten away with a few infidelities
and sure a few got away from me too
in this life search to arrive at or at least epitomize a scripture
built freely from perceptions and fellow outsiders
most recently the discovery that all public transpo in milan is free or can be
—not even b/c you can't pay but b/c you can't find where to pay—
or once upon a long ago copping a bag of dirt my first night in paris
or the machine gun alarm stealing from a field of weed in belize
totaling a bmw in pensacola
nights in drag in new orleans   lifted purses full of illicit prescriptions
smoke rising from an epic joint on top of the temple of the lost world
above the howler monkeys' canopy during golden hour
the most religious experience I've ever percieved
—lemme tell you raul's rose garden got alot of thorns
& you don't want the mississippi treatment in orleans parish prison—
better off pissing on the panthéon after dine-n-dashing le select
successfully bribing the cops out of a dui in quito
or getting kicked out of the entire town of canoa
a blur of junk in jakarta—have I even been to jakarta?
certainly syringes in the ass in ustica
from maria my romanian nursemaid
after taking a bends hit cave diving
sure I've browned out in brooklyn
yawping ferlinghetti on a subway car
dedicated to all the vanished street performers
unknowingly in front of students
slurring beside my enduring buddy darren
which reminds me   I can continue

definitely taunted mortality too many times to fully litany
taking the train to san sebastian with only
14 bottles of wine, a beach towel, and a bathing suit
afterwards buying hashish in a cathedral confessional
eventual pursuit and expulsion by security from a radiohead show
for refusing to quit sailing to the moon
insistent on hiking up a mtn then slipping off a 20-meter cliff
to certain drunken demise
on the fracturing waves and crags
before darren gave me the best shove I've ever received
yesterday a dutch emt asked me if I ever saved a life
and I told him well not technically
I've helped a friend or fellow diver with a few safe ascents and descents
prevented the use of some improperly used equipment
separated a few fights that may have escalated
and certainly fellated my licks along the way
or flocked the fuck away from trouble of every color that can be mixed
survival is its own impressionist masterpiece
all these little green and brown dots resembling the home of a park or bench
some scene made from making scenes or avoiding them
the getaway monet worth a hundred million or more
a painstaking trophy of unsustainability
of throwing yourself away into the only world that was offered

nederland alternative endings

    i.

the getaway   is   the hatching
the creeping months
of whispers
of decisive indecision
and late night walks
with your lover
the necessity of beginning to declare
what was dear to me
now dead to me
the dispossession of possessions
giving away all paraphernalia
stuffing cash into the mattress
awaiting the tools, tolls, and coitus
for the pallet to turn piñata
the favors called in
the stash of prescriptions
the passport photo pose
hustling online legal documents
the greedy details that keep you going
abroad like the silhouettes of sailboats
in parallax sunset as you attempt
to settle in the mist of getaway

ii.

(vent's dormant   playing a crooked world straight
beleaguered impotence of immigrants
                              divided by fissures in the system
a form of seventh extinction)

iii.

the getaway is ripe for tessalated mistakes
all paintings, promises, delivered or undelivered
tiny bottles of truffle oil hidden in your parents' pantry
muffulettas to go
a quaking canine to import something blues from home
frantic packing   goodbyes nourished on dwindling time
boots, belts, and bottles of basil hayden falling out the trunk
a few desperate final acts of subversion
dug a mass grave for maga hats in dulles
then   suspension of reality   flight
afterwards you arrive to beautiful stumbles
familiar surprises and unfamiliar contradictions
waterways of unpronounceable names
you scan train passengers for a hint of friend
but it's mostly headphones, yourself included
you get a small job mainly to get out of bed
then you realize—sans gunpoint—
the university is more dependency than the dream
they are saying this country is now polluted

which defeats your intention of cleaning up
the land you soil   if not your act
                                    to trick the slyest of all:
life—such an escape artist metamorphosis
this not yet universe   an escher of stunts
we excuse everything   drafting from square one

          iv.

(insist anyway
      you sluice)

another city lights pilgrimage

frisco, always a topshelf getaway destination
this time, from december and the dutchies—
as we've come to affectionately
and not-so-affectionately call them
like most things said, read, or unsaid
it really just depends on the tone
a promising two nights in a real city
(pardon the air of superiority; it's only
a retort from a recent lowly immigrant)
arriving directly from drinks at stanford
to a bought room at the hyatt regency
on embarcadero, I check in to a free sierra
not a bad city start as city starts go
I change clothes to something more street
more comfy, more meant for walking
north beach in december and I'm off
alone, it's as simple as that
sidewalk footsteps insinuate skyscrape—
the transamerica pyramid always gets me
on the return, a 48-story of futurist
brutalism, a behemoth I can't help
but ankle in awe, yet slight going out
my mission is simple and three-fold:
first, an authentic bowl of pho, then
buy *little boy*, ferlinghetti's newest book
a memoir veiled novel but all poem
direct from my elder's open mouth
(booksellers gettable until midnight!) and

end by beginning the book with drinks at vesuvio
creasing a brand new crystal ball of a book
running freely in the words in a crowd
hence the hills couldn't stop my fresh feet
and next thing I know I see broadway's
neon signs shining striptease brighter
and more unwavering than any standard
as of late   I think about endurance
esp the seedy persuasion and wonder
if us low of the low—strippers and junkies
to which many would include beat poets, aren't
actually still on-to something   how this street stands
as tall as any sky-fracker in the financial
I see city lights and I can't contain myself
skipping in like a schoolchild who already
has a friend on the first day of first grade
lawrence, lawrence, where are you?
ready or not... given I've turned preadolescent
the bespectacled bookworm behind the counter
fails to capture my attention
I dart to the city lights stacks
instantly finding the legendary *HOWL*
I flip to the footnote
allen's holy of holies
the ASSHOLE
delight in impure jubilation!
I put it back only to spot an old baltimore friend
city lights put out madison smart bell's latest
now there's a contemporary that writes cities!
make a mental note to scoop up that one

when I'm flush again, having skipped the country
and not received a full check since august
WTF no lawrence front and city center?
guess I'll have to comb the other stacks
scouring—a little desperately I might add—
(my belly empty with the exception of cheers)
the shelves of recently-released fiction
close to the register, I sense I had forgotten
my safety net headphones intentionally
craving an urban earful these two short days
surely a dangerous poem or two to overhear
given I grew up in bookstores and libraries
knew the alphabet, title, even author this hunt
must just be a masochist's gratification delay or
maybe it was to overhear the following exchange:
a buttoned-up young man walks up to the purple-haired girl
at the city lights register and asks innocently about the bookstore
who they were, have they been here long   *this should be fun*
"uh, we're famous," she responds. "have you ever heard of *HOWL*?"
...*really lady, you start with ginsberg, instead of lawrence*
and don't even say ginsberg's name...
"haven't" he concedes with a sausalito smile
"there was like an obscenity case against it that went
to the supreme court." "oh," our bashful suitor offers
"so do you have any books about business?"
oh shit   buffoon   she's going to really flog you now
instead, kindly and without condescension she says:
"um no, we're not that kind of bookstore"
by the time our mba politely thanks her and leaves
I'm done eavesdropping and I've found

ferlinghetti, published by doubleday!
I rush to the register to purchase
and to my dismay   not a nod
comment or little praise
about the appropriateness
of the selection given the setting   nada
should I offer a quip, code of being in the know?
just the old receipt and bag query, both refused
I had found the friend I came for
and we were already chasing each other to the bar
alas, poor vesuvio, brimming with tourists
besides myself and silicon sleaze   so much so
two friends that have met but never shared life stories
could barely find a nook to get down to the deets
upstairs was out of the question so order first
"two sierras," I shout, "and close me out"
dodging tech metaphors like *pipelines* and *ecosystems*
we find the corner of corners at the bar, waiting
and meant to be   good and hoppy I tackle all the front
and back matter, and finally settle down to listen
to a last hero standing's unbelievable story
imbuing his mind myth of coney island
origin of love where his immigrant parents met
crashed bumper cars and started a family of five
mother couldn't afford after father died
so the kid was whisked off to france by a rich aunt
only to wind up back in a u.s. orphanage from whence
your boy manned up to command sub destroyers
in the dday invasion of normandy continuing to wander nagaski
7 days after "fat boy" dropped apocalypse

making him instant pacifist—not to mention
studying at chapel hill and doctorate in 3 years in paris
what a tale and what a tail to tell it with? *wink wink.*
30 pages deep the beer emptied and my stomach in need
of a healthier brew plus it was too loud for the intimacy
we required anyway   the spell broken and I had proved my tiny rebellion
by reading at a packed bar, once and again literally literary
leaving I notice some ruffians in kerouac alley smoking
with acoustic guitars but I have no urge to join
their little band   I peek back inside city lights and the
young woman working is tapping her phone   expected
I confess I too have tapped between pages
sending vesuvio drunk texts to andrei, bill
and dewitt, not to mention beseeching google maps to improve
my chances of finding the best of nearby broths
the trafficked street silent, holy, I look up, knowing ferlinghetti
in the flesh is probably in bed above me   again, where, precisely
I'm not sure   I try to decipher the lights   which windows
likely residential   search the possibilities for his abode—
there's a third floor one that looks promising—and if perchance
he's up, making a trip to the restroom as old men tend to regularly do
I decide maybe the doors are a better strategy
really only two entrances that could be his threshold:
one on columbus or this other one on grant
maybe a tiny one on broadway but I'm not betting on it
there's less than ten buzzers between them
*should I just press each one? start with this one
glowing faint orange in front of me?* I read names
on the buzzer boxes   poets love mail   we may be the last
on that front too, besides all these amazon packages

another deduction   a 100-year-old bookseller probably
isn't spending too much time shopping online
there's a nonsense-moniker sounding name that sorta jives
with beat sensibility   *should I ring?*   the temptation
is edenic   I hear andrei in the window
at the molly's at the market of my mind
saying: "you want to meet a poet? go ring their doorbell."
but I can't force myself to do it
bug the old man   who knows his condition when woken
(I know mine) how lucid he'd be, if he would even receive me
I abandon my eyes, still scanning the dim windows above
imagine our meeting   two italian-american poets
one still chasing the dream and one founded one
interpreting melodies in unison or more likely disagreeing
we could have that drink or smoke together
what would he advise me?   what would I read him?
I abandon the what-might-be-my-last-chance
fantasy of great-poetic-grandfather
who wrote the only book of *poetry* with over a million copies in print
AND fucking BELLOWED out ginsberg's "famous" *HOWL*
for all to hear
for all to read
I stash his fresh words in my jacket pocket
that's enough for me
for now
and for all time
together
we will go
searching for warmth and spice

moped morse code

engines every morning
outside my window:
rev
long dash
dot dot
short dash
stop
bromfiets
pass
swerve
hit the speed bump
off stop
some ciphers smoother electric
others dilapidated hollow mufflers
clanging tin disintegrating
drum in ear
where slumber still urges
the rattles of the bicycles
over the stone roads
even the pedaling
becomes a character
in this communicative commute
the routine
disturbs me
enough to rise
as I have work to get to too
but first

a tiny getaway
to fill my tea and a page
amidst all their indecipherable racket
chainsaw mopeds deforesting
their provincial streets

Porch Beers VS. the Bore of Existential Fears

What are our friends in New Orleans doing right now?

That's the question I ask Sarah sometimes
after a few beers on the porch.
Tonight, as I crack the fourth. Sarah, her second.

For a moment she just rocks on the swing—smiles
and sips her Peroni. Sips again.

I suggest we make it a game—play pretend.

Sarah decides she'll take Jordan and Veronica.
I opt for Adrian and Darcy.

Adrian prepares lasagna. His hands zombie-hover
above boiling noodles. Darcy in the den
prepares Sunday's sermon on the joy of creativity.

Jordan is mixing a stiff martini in a mason jar.
Veronica shimmies over with two fat olives; plops
them in. Gives his ass a pat.

The game goes on like this for maybe 10 minutes.

A few friends are drunk, more than one
sporting a ragged pair of assless chaps—none
getting away with anything we wouldn't.

We swallow a long drink—both of us slow
and deliberate—like a song had insisted we do it.

I check our phones to see which has the most life;
put on the Spotify playlist Sarah made
for Halloween—our last in New Orleans.

Depeche Mode's "Ghost" creeps up and we're out
of beers. I haunt the house for something darker.

A spent can becomes an easy ashtray.
On nights like this we burn through a whole pack
with little shame. I mention Vince, who
always says *scags* for cigarettes.

But Vince just moved to Delft maybe a month ago.
He can't be a part of our little game.

What the hell's Vince doing in Delft? I ask anyway.

Yeah—or Peyton and Ryan in Richmond?
Sarah asks, grabbing the bottle before I'm ready
to give it up. But we've both had enough.

VI. THE DAMPEST OF SPIRITS

one puddle

in particular
makes my
rainy days

most days
it's the mere
formed in
the middle
of the bike
path under
construction
heading to
campus

and away
from delft's
center city
canal's
southern
drain

the dampest
of spirits
is no match
for crossing
this puddle

as we speed
in packs
like sunk rats
to face our duties
and whatever
gnaws on us

there's a moment
in passing
where everyone
secretly
delighted
slows down

pulls their feet
off the pedals
(some even rise!)
as if about to float
and coasts
out of their
brooding into
the inevitable
splashing
out of
personal
paths

we
acknowledge
our own role
in
jeopardy
and
the oncomer
making
us
all kin
in our brief exodus
from everything

~getting away with everything

Now When I am

Now when I'm walking around
Kenyon College I'm thinking of that
Frank O'Hara poem the one
about how funny it would be if we
shit just once a week because it's raining
here not cats and dogs I don't know
if I've ever said it's raining cats and dogs
if I said something like that now
I'd say skunks and spiders
that's what I have in my head right now
I have spiders in my head spiders
because Andy said the other night that
he's always looking out for spiders
around here then later I saw
a web while we smoked on the porch
outside the O'Connor house and I
mentioned it to him said better look out
and pointed at the web which
had no spider just a bug I don't know
the name of and when I pointed
to the web I remembered remembering
to tell him I saw a spider on Brad
at the bar the other night it was sort of
still in a way that made it seem lost
and surely it was so I cupped it
in my palm carried it out into the drizzle
now it's raining again it wasn't
when I saw that skunk with Geoff

and Jenn the skunk that slid its way
toward us yesterday afternoon
when the sun peeked out and surely it
felt liberated in that flash of
warmth like us must have when it rose
to sniff the air then skunked
off to sniff other air other air not wet
with rain it wasn't raining then but now
it's raining again harder than
before and now I'm thinking of that
Frank poem that particular one because
that's when I think I got Frank
the first time I mean really got him
when I was on the phone with him
he might've said alone in my apartment
alone in a new city a new state
with no one to call up to get lunch with
it was raining and my apartment
was dark like I like it when I'm reading
the dark that scares my wife
that tells her to tell me I'll go blind
maybe I don't like it maybe I just forget
to turn on a light but really
there's something about that kind
of natural light that gray middle-of-the-
day-rain-light through the blinds
it makes you feel like you're in a cabin
on a ship going somewhere
exotic and that's the kind of rain now
the kind of light walking around

Kenyon through the rain on the way
to lunch at the deli where I have a bagel
and lox that I almost finish before
a couple folks show up I can't remember
their names I'm sad I can't remember
their names but happy they join me
and we talk about potato chips and tattoos
music and movies and maybe that's
when Andy joins us maybe that's when we
start in about movies and now I'm
thinking of Frank again who loved movies
who I like to think loved the rain
and sun the same that maybe that kind
of thing just kind of killed him you know
but now alive sitting down for lunch
at the deli now we are in love
with *Birdman* with talking about *Birdman*
with *Whiplash* with ends of things
we're so in love with the ends of things
the ends of movies but the ends of
other things we don't talk about I can tell
we're in love with those things too
but when we leave we all leave separately
split up take off at different times
like airplanes lined up on a runway but all
going to the same place and where
I want to go is that old church on the hill
not because it's beautiful it is but I'm
thinking of Frank that first poem I fell in
love with that first one I called up

on the phone had lunch with when it was
raining and my apartment was dark
and I was alone and now walking through
Kenyon in that kind of rain I remember
he ended the poem with a Sunday
and a church and a plop and I ended it with
a laugh and loved the beginning
and the end of something the same
and maybe got hungry enough to get out
in the rain to get some lunch or something
but now after just having lunch maybe
now I'll go check out the church on the hill
to see what the lighting inside is like

stations of the crossed

saw a belly hanging out
of a slob on the train
passed out all the way
from delft
to amsterdam playing
the whole car
rap over his speakerphone
(common in the states
but here it stands out)

a young couple reunited
dancing in the crowded
airport train depot
an infant straddled
between them
exceeding the spirit
of carols streaming
from a less festive display

a dreadlocked dude
face-timing with his girl
enjoying the stinkiest
landfill of onions, frites
and mayonnaise
like a last supper
and conjugal visit

a millennial band of
merry travelers
singing "take me home
country roads..."
gathered around
the station's
grand piano
a refrain I change
to dedicate
to my dog and
croon to no one
in particular
pretty regularly
but it took this
chorus to remind
me of the good
ol original
john denver

and there's me
still implicated
sneaking in 1st class
when 2nd gets full
with a notepad, pen
and a coat full
of heinekens
always ready to flee

I've never gotten caught
yet to be fined
but I'm writing
this book
so there's
an ongoing
hope

The New Human Within

Now as I think I must become
a new human I'm in New Orleans
in line at Breaux Mart
thinking only a city like this would have
a store named Breaux Mart
as the oblivious yet pissed off cashier calls
whoever she calls to check
the price of a tomato a shopper
three shoppers ahead of me has placed
in front of her as I wonder
after all that's happened why people still
bother to pick the right
tomato and in the same sky so many egrets
flying above the ugly bayou
I'll drive by on my way home and now
I never turn on my radio
in my car because NPR harks on about
depression and bombs and
to anyone out there Monday means murder
some poor fuck named Tom
but I just used *harks* because it sounds safe
and I am my best self now
as I take this nuclear breath and I'm not
Tom and I won't be afraid
of a shootout because there's no tomato
in my cart and on the way home
again not for a minute will I tune in

roaming free blues / a systemic murder ballad

what kind of impossible
restructuring do we
really need
to release
non-violent drug
offenders
and petty criminals
those whose imprisonment
has more to do
with impoverishment
or color
and
to cast some stones
and incarcerate
the grayscale
spectrum
of stalkers
and sex abusers
that never seem
to face any
consequences
from on high
in fact full
of direst cruelty
crowns on
bigots and creeps
think 2019
is their year

encouraged by
oval approval
and the silent
and powerless
resignation
of their prey
that has made
america a great place
to roam   for them
and in this year alone
no less than four women
in universities—have told me
and I'd bet more
than the vast majority
esp knowing the service industry—
have been stalked, harassed
or worse by someone
who will not even
get a puny slap
on their sturdy
slime-ridden wrists
an impregnable figure
daily tormenting
unless one resorts to
hiding at home
these swine are ruins
and ruin is a specialized
knowledge esp
in institutions
but worse

they have the rules
and state authority shares
their disposition
let freedom ruin
this is a lament
for the unjust
treatment of
more than
our wives
mothers
daughters
this is a call
to end this curse
of acceptance
and poisoned authority
all too prevalent
throughout our planet
to topple sexed power
& annihilate the status quo

Unrepentant Caverns

Now I'm in New Orleans drifting off
in a private school's chapel service
holding a thought that only
god is godless as the monstrously large
organ pipes whine behind me
when I imagine a passenger plane
crashing through the boringly bat-less
rafters where the organ pipes rise
toward the vaulted ceiling's polished
wood at back of the chapel
and I'm reminded how much the pipes
look like stalagmites maybe fingers
of stone fingers with so many
knobby knuckles it's as if they belong
to an ancient witch buried
beneath a cave's dream so long ago
somehow they have grown
so monstrously large a massive hand
has managed to crack through
the stone floor only to always point up
and I wonder how it would feel
to always be pointing to be in one place
forever pointing up toward what
will always point down and
now when I slide my own fingers over
shifty shapes lining the floor
of my failing memory I remember
every strange finger that I saw glisten

with freshwater dripping
from the roof of the cave I toured once
at Silver Dollar City when I was
a kid and now when I'm remembering
how weird it was a cave was hidden
under an amusement park
that 300 ft above where the stalactites
dripped their years of slow drips
down from the dark ceiling was the roar
of rollercoasters so many screams
I remember how weird it was
no one said a thing about how weird
it was that the tour guide
just kept pointing up at all the glistening
stone like tiny lights clicking
infinitely on and off and when I recall
the cold of that cave it's a breath
on the back of my neck but now when
I shift in my seat the imagined
passenger plane crashes again big white
nose first through the bat-less
rafters and now as the wood splinters
down over the crowd of students
and teachers I have one of those out-of-
body experiences I guess
because I'm floating out over the pew
full of singing kids and I see
myself down there sitting song-less
sucking cinnamon Altoids two at a time
and as the charming priest

is beginning his sermon on the dangers
of drugs the plane no one
notices continues crashing through slow-
motion-style without sound
and now as I'm not a bit surprised how
suddenly my wingspan is
unbelievable how easy learning to fly is
I'm back in the pew again
sitting with the singing kids again
and I can't see myself fly up there ready
to catch the plane in my palm
to save all the oblivious kids from all
their invisible screams and
now the priest pauses a priestly
pause to sharpen his long tongue against
the kids as the pulpit becomes
a box of bats that fly up to hang from
the rafters I'm so still I feel
I've always been a finger made of stone

sacred in sacred out

yet another lazy sunday
exclaiming the lord's name in vain

gettin away
from god
for many a young person
is the premiere struggle

in reverence
in reference

when all the metaphors
we inherited
cease
to make you believe
or yearn for the shepherd
of sight in order to find
a spiritual king's dominion

so you abandon the words first
and then the flock
which often pits you
against your own parents
self-compelled jailers of beliefs
their child's personal creators
and saviors and while I've never
had the pain of raising a human
volunteering my child to list

every sin for an education
is a helluva trade

I believe in the line
a poet's ramblings to reach
farther into this world and the next
converse with the living and the dead
instead of taking up a collection
or asserting some authority
hence I refuse most institutions
formed to spread or profit
from a particular dogma
and personally I'll always have
more respect for people that
fight religion than follow it

to me there's more god
in the peter moment
the thrice denial
a predicted act of cowardice
as commonly interpreted
but there's something exceptional
lingering there—more than the weakness
which jesus shared asking to be spared—
of not following any prophet or god
to battle nor death
a refusal of association
and martyrs
working out their lines

lately I place less emphasis on my denials
I've come to grips with us
in terms of physics
entirely as energy or spirit
the collective unconscious
recycling souls
in the solar expanse
an image of our age
a conception I hope you deny

Will the Real Secret Agent Please Stand Up?

Now when I'm wishing I could slip back
into an old loneliness I'm back
in New Orleans back to the first year there
walking back to the corner
coffee shop again when I remember
it's Easter as a swarm of flowery dresses
and fancy ties crowd to cross
Magazine as I look down at my dirty shirt
the one with the nerdy cat
sporting specs the one I've worn for days
lazy-haunting the house and I'm
reminded how much of a mess I become
when Sarah's gone and Sarah's
gone to Paris but now I see our neighbors
eating brunch outside Gott Gourmet
I remember the pile of mail
I left for them when I housesat while they
were gone to Florida and now
they thank me for the mail ask me to join
but I'm trying to get good at being
alone I've been trying to get good at being
alone for the past 24 hours
watching the entire first season of *24*
on Netflix so I feel like a zombie
could really use their company but I say
thanks no sorry I've got work
and take off toward the corner coffee shop
but it's closed for Easter so I go

to Starbucks and order whatever they call
the biggest black coffee they've got
take it back to the empty patio
it's cold out but I stay anyway I remember
that Sarah's seven hours ahead
can call me up maybe if she isn't in bed
if I'm logged on to the free Wi-Fi
but when I look away from messing with
the settings on my phone
this beefy white guy dressed in black
cap black shirt black pants black
socks black shoes walks through the patio
and I imagine he must be
a terrorist that he's holding my neighbors
hostage that somewhere in Paris
his people have Sarah tied to a chair and
now here he is with the phone
he'll hold up to my ear so I can hear her
voice on the far-away phone
held up to her to confirm she's safe before
he snatches it back before he says
they'll slit her pretty throat now if I don't
allow them to implement me
in their plan to kill the president and when
I look up again he's gone inside
I'm alone again on the cold patio hoping
my text to Sarah will send
before it's too late to say goodnight

mae's-en-scène

also known as "the club"
a once smoke-filled
petri dish of new orleans
stepping in for the first time
as a youngun conjured
the enchanted scene
from *star wars: a new hope*
when obi wan takes luke
to the space bar to find a pirate
the drunken jazz, gambling
women, and fights spilling
outside we never tired of
that reflective glass door
framed yellow and black portal
altered time after crossing
the glow of the namesake orange
neon on magazine
and napoleon
pushing the stiffest drinks
you can find for $1
open 24/7, 3-6-5
it never closed
it stood to bewitch
its visitors & regulars alike
and in a year or two
it transcended to "our bar"
if you went early enough
you could have drinks

with miss mae herself
who would cut your ass
if you disrupted her jeopardy
so you held your answers
like you had the hiccups
miss mae had a sandy mullet of curls
and smoked winstons with a chain
thick enough she could anchor
in the deep sea
legend has it
she was a working girl
that bought her way out
then bought this dive
across from the police station
it was assumed she had dirt
on the entire town, especially them
running this type of establishment
on their front lawn
mae never lifted a finger
except to ash but she
often raised her voice
she would come in
(sometimes with a crew) sip
greyhounds, smoke, shush us, and watch tv
originally mae's was further uptown
on magazine a location now called st. joe's
both had reputations for underage drinking
hence why we came
and kept coming
but everybody went to mae's

musicians, locals, cooks, dealers
hobos, college students,
even the cops in street clothes
it was the closest spot
to tipitina's to get cheap drinks
so before or after shows
an influx of pre or post gamers
and random locals
many costumed for one excuse or none
caused the club to ebb and flow
out of the side entrance
between the second pool
and foosball table
a door would swing wide open
and people would spill onto
the sidewalk cars parked
all over smoking, puking
laughing, pissing
fighting, crying, fucking
name any gerund
at night we spilled into the darker
shadows below the oaks' armpits
sitting on the stoops of mansions
to get our mind right
a reefer break as kermit
still says before he ends his first set
during mardi gras the place
transformed into an atomic
bomb shelter for boozing
wells lined with lead

all the tables, chairs, and games
removed to solely sling
and offer a floor to piss on
for hordes of shoulder to shoulder
parade goers
now this lyric turns litany
to remember our undoing
one of infinite corners
our edge of dinge
twisted in the club's heyday:

occasionally playing pool
with hiram both drunk
not even looking at the table
while shooting and beating
people way better than us
which would drive opponents mad

sneaking girls
and friends
without fakes
through the side door

sweet and gray
bassist walter payton
an old gentleman steady sippin
some brown on the video poker
machines telling me and em
how he can only play with
his eyes closed

every time he saw us
he'd use the line
you must be named michael
because she's an angel

tying one on by
slamming madrases or heinekens
before or after countless
shows at tips: tim reynolds, walter wolfman,
fats domino, wilco, les claypool, george clinton
ivan neville's dumpstaphunk,
karl denson's late night shows
that didn't start until 2 am
and let out well after sunrise

stumbling home in daylight
thru saturday yard sales
uptown on our way home picking up
a trinket to forget & find in the afternoon

cooks in checks screaming:
how long black out?
walking in the front door
demanding waiters
with pockets full of tips
provide drinks
at the cheapest
bar in town

buying drinks for any stranger
ever because it was only $1

meetings with dreadlocked swamp thing
to buy bubblegum kush which he imported from cali
and hid in a sock on his silver crotch rocket
he would ride nightly to the club and back
from the 9th ward

a few times I hopped on back to get home to mae's
after a halloween panic show or pinball absinthe orgy on desire st
we took off   headless horseman on an interstellar chariot

eventually befriending him to the point
where he arranged a 6 ft. tank of nitrous
as a thanksgiving party favor beside the turkey fryer

wild man pulling a knife on darren
by the jukebox

running the foos table
playin $25 per ball
against ben and yoda

sprinting out the side door
vomiting in the trash can outside
sometimes not making it
but always returning
and ordering a heineken

buying shots after insults
because it was cheaper and easier
to ruin an enemy with drink

stumbling to sav-a-center
once the clock read 4:44
to buy bagels, champagne
and astroglide

finding a tulane friend
passed out on the raised toilet
behind the saloon doors
his pants down with bag of blow
and key plow raised

a dealer and dear friend
selling me a car for a $1 and a drink
so 2 drinks

friends debating on hooking up friends
because they peed themselves
the evidence darkened designer skirts or shorts

befriending all the bartenders
smiling al & john, who went on to do porno
post katrina days, which seemed a demotion
compared to manning the helm of mae's

the year we didn't pay for a drink

maybe we bartered a bit
there was no spoken agreement

leaving with G to get inked
or push a portapotty
over in the street

a cajun cook eating a tourist out
in the back of a united cab
running in the driveway with a crowd
cheering him on

walker belligerently strolling into the police
station demanding his car was stolen
only to find it the next day parked outside

walter drunkenly wrestling nicole
in piles of parade trash
for what seemed like hours
on the neutral ground
out front as firetrucks and prisoners
with rakes cleaned up after our first lundi gras bbq

G snapping a pool stick over his leg
and plunging out the side door
in frustration
because he didn't punch someone
who likely deserved it

getting in a limo with strippers from shreveport

going at it on the pool table with a more-tempting
-than-them promise of unending bottles
of budweiser & jagermeister
drifting uptown, downtown, st. charles, to the fly
eventually freebasing in audubon
in the weedless hours of morning
before they went back and woke up
wild man with a lap dance claiming
he looked just like her son

getting handled by an off duty pig
smashing my face in the concrete stairs
held tight in hammer lock until al talked him off me
all because I had a pocket knife from painting
visibly hated his presence and may have told him

teasing hiram about decorating a wheelbarrow
with purple, gold, and green mardi gras beads
for dumping his overnight stays back on the corner of mae's

alternate endings
     between mae's and delmonico
or mae's and theo's
    walk-in with molly
        to milan lounge
or the public storage
  practice space
     marengo moonlight
       back from the berumda triangle
on any other given night

~getting away with everything

partying or working
a negligible difference
more accurately a combination

flooding our guts past curfew
with the national guard
& fbi patrolling the streets
in their hummers & suburbans
armed to the teeth

endless verbal contests
from worst pick up lines
to best fetishes
the mardi gras day challenge
walker and dr payne almost
made it 24 hours straight
drinking there
I returned twice
sleeping in between
the same timeframe

throwing yourself out
of the bar by the collar
because no one else would

all the quotidian bar shit
the countless recounts
of debauchery and shenanigans
the jukebox favorites
"sweet leaf" x 3

getting kicked out
not remembering why
coming back dirty or clean the next day
no apology   no questions asked
no reward but the treasured hours
                    we can't remember
of friends   and feeling
                    alive and fucked up
immune to
mistakes washed away in the mississippi

~getting away with everything

I'm the Kingpin in the City of My Sad Song

Now as I'm lamenting everything
I'm in New Orleans crying
again at Kingpin when
this guy in a pea coat walks in and
shoves between me and Sarah
so he can elbow the bar
and now when I'm asking myself
if he can see I'm crying
if he can tell that I'm the kingpin
in the city of my sad song
I stop crying and start to want
a White Russian because
the guy in the pea coat orders two
White Russians and I don't
think I've had a White Russian
for something like ten years
so I say we'll take two of those too
without asking Sarah
if she wants one and now she says
she doesn't want one
but I know it's one of those times
when I can't take back
anything that I can't just change
my order after having
cried at Kingpin because it's also
one of those kinds of times
so I tell Sarah I'll just drink hers
and she smiles and says ok

and gets up to go to the bathroom
and I start to go weak
in my knees when she leaves
though I'm sitting down
and now when I stare at the cooler
of imports I almost cry again
but the TV hanging above the bar
for some reason looks like
the head of an alien my very own
Sigourney Weaver has
hunted down because she knows
I'm the kingpin in the city
of my sad song and will always be

honestly

leaving new orleans
was getting away from
getting away with everything
and I know you felt now-or-never-compelled to do the same
and now we must exorcise the doubt of our chances of assimilating back to normal
society even if you increased your stay and survival   same as me
but hey one good thing is I'm not sure we'd have the distance
to stare into this puddle reflection still in the driver seats in this reckless hearse
swerving
no place will ever be the same
                    and neither will we
for worst or utmost we believe in this swathe here
and caterpillars, our toast to those lost taking the protean risk
so our real getaway—if we get everything—swears more colors and wings
than we can conjure up in carnival   and words remain our rootwork
there are other muses to love   most kill   rob   or pollute you less
                    promise a burst   a flutter
as opposed to tragic embryos sinking in quicksand
(then again amsterdam is a short train ride away and thibodeaux is coming next week)

street food nude

maybe once in montañita
high on conch & cocaine
a front cabana dinner
strip jenga in the sand
before the night's bonfire where
the german and argentinian
girls—after enjoying our joints—
proved more interested
in the ecuadorian locals
than any of our claims
   or maybe twice in cabo
slurping raw clams & limons
preceded then chased
by ice chests of pacifico
after being frightened
& relieved in a long shower
sharing soap with a friend
as I mistook
a yellowfin fishing injury
for a mermaid std
   certainly a delusion in italy
for this graduate student
staying in a castle
outside of dead man's tower
overlooking the adriatic
and ionian seas consummate
their affair   a daily fling
in santa maria di leuca

after diving my buddy and I
frequented the same stand
in the market for rotisserie
chicken on a spit dripping
fat onto the potatoes below
two big bottles of heineken
apiece behind the counter
was always the mother
who welcomed us warmly
and her shy vision of a daughter
whose presence was as piercing
as the fares of her family
face that launched 1,000 spits
she beset our quotidian orbits
we termed her the chicken girl
an unworthy label not reflecting
our romantic estimation of her
for far lesser beauty ruined
many far finer men   after a few days
we had a habit   of stalling
and juggling the football
with her baby brother
we never noticed a father
and surely we assumed   if there was one
he'd have chased us off already
we imagined scenarios
poor widowed or abandoned
and this fact only increased
our infatuation   soon my fantasies
increased in inebriated complexity

including dropping out of grad school
marrying this girl   starting a family
opening a dive shop and helping
run the family roitisserie
feasting on 7 fishes christmas eve on sea cliffs
when I realized I didn't know what I was more
attracted to   this bella to be my everything
or the second chance to have an italian mother
mother me   I knew it was time to leave

Sharing a Smoke

—*for Michelle*

Now that I'm getting away with all
I can really hope to as I smoke my last
Christmas cigarette in my mother's
garage messy with broken-down
boxes and empty paint cans before
heading north to Illinois I imagine you
sitting in that dark three-car garage
you often mentioned in your long-
fingered letters the archive of emails
I've been excavating in short trips
between short trips to the coffee shop
the liquor store on the county line
the graveyard all the light always seen
the new mall where most folks
in this small Arkansas town tow home
something like god in plastic bags
to pile beneath twinkling trees
because when there is no atonement
for how small everything will
inevitably become it drives me to
smoke another get in just one last drag
before attempting again to leave
behind what always travels with me
so now as I light another I remember
again that pile of ashes it seems
we both knew needed sifting for seeds

to just keep going a bit longer
even though only you gave it a name
put it in a book but when I see you
alone in that garage that dark garage
alone in front of that massive fan
saving you from the mean Florida heat
even though you are gone you
are growing larger behind the screen
you behind the light of your laptop
aglow with each flick of your cigarette
the used butts piling up beside you
an unlikely totem a song for giving up
everything else you said but I wish
we could share a smoke instead of this

northern high noon

how to postpone a duel
move from southern saloons
to northern wooden taverns
above the 52nd parallel
sun's azimuth
off to the side
where high noon
if you're lucky
looks like
the 10am LA
morning sun
sweating
is rare
for suspects
and even folks
on the lam
run outside
or call in sick
from work
to get some sun
you could wait
around most
of the year
for said climax
to come
miss it mistakenly
if you saw
the white faint glow

that never achieves
blazing this far
away from
the equator
a heated laissez
place more
suited for bandits
and bothering
showdowns
and disasters
going down
crimes and passions
and crimes of passion
here a cold rotated egress
shadowless
which only accentuates
the former warmth of all
the getting aways
all the everythings
all the high noons
under a burning sun
you stepped outside
they didn't bury you

The Obligation to Meaning

Now as my dog as always gets
away with everything I ask myself
if he has actually learned
to speak in some supernatural flash
of knowledge as he pauses
after an initial whimper and I think
I hear him say he's beginning
a new poem and that *pit
of plum sitting on book* is the first
line and now when I am
wincing at this my wife says
very matter-of-factly that he's just
engaging with the poetic
possibilities of everyday life then
twirls her finger in her hair
for a bit before stopping to inspect
the split-ends and now when
I say *OK* to myself and leave them
both to the sheeted furniture
of their obligations to meaning then
sink into the unmade bed
of mine I hear a horn honk outside
and just like that my dog
is back to barking and now when
he turns his thoughts inward
like a turned-off TV and now when
he cries out for the lost ones

among us and now when he paws
at the stuffed snake stuck
under the couch for something like
a year he promptly forgets
about the beginning of the poem

raised as a barrel in the cellar

a damp incantation to wake
during a lucid nightmare
or uttered to stave off
the spontaneous fermentation of ghosts
in a haunted hideaway of a world war
also used as a lament for the lamentless
hence its inclusion in the present collection
in 18 mardi gras I solidified my childishness forever
the 19th I am apprehended by some stowaway adult in me
who guarantees if I don't starve for at least this one
I'll never be able to age this fantasy
there are older cellars
more bulbous barrels
not to mention different libations anthems and dances
to learn by pouring yourself into
the span of our soul's storage
a shelf life of mystery which yearns for company and home
as well as delivery from the status quo into the unknown
the angel's share, a deserved disappearance
sips sacrifice everything
we getaway in gulps
our contents all catalyst
missing mardi gras blues
try to tell myself mardi gras is a state of mind
given ubiquitous purple gold and green
been replaced with daily wind, rain, and grey
I swear, at least sisyphus, all this time
was getting stoned on a mountain

a real punishment would have been
a permanent bicycle commute in dutch winter
so turn on the WWOZ to drown out all the doubt
pour some sequin wine
get out our favorite throws
no costumes claiming the house
no glue gun to the head this year
no ham hocks or turkey necks smoked in the street
no stealing muffulettas or chicken wings
with an improvised doggie bag
from some random party
I try to think of the filthiest thing available to eat:
kapsalon, a rotterdam invention, meaning "hairdresser"
doner toppings over gouda cheese fries
before heading out to procure the grease feast
we play a motivation round of "iko iko" and "indian red"
I don the tasteful naked nymph button-down I found
in goodwill decades ago and it's provided
every muses since
my two and four-legged angels
and I strut the medieval streets
feign a hoot and holler
that really doesn't outweigh the dutch frat boys
on a given saturday but we make a scene or three
all in the name of the day
after a jenever tasting
miraculously we find a small band of brass and a snare to follow
about 20 catholic dutchies drunk with LEDs making a racket
marching around city center waving colors
below dark gothic towers and protestant grimaces

from the wealthy apartments above
although not as many, a few admirers
rush to the windows and doorways
swaying all smiles and waves
mostly children really but a few parents too
reminding me: wherever you go
go in joy   raise spirits
form a getaway parade
        the otherwise
from gloomy days
find your people
tell them everything
if for only an hour
before we all disperse into the dark

The New Bird Sings

Now as I listen to what
we've been calling *the new bird*
sing what sounds like *cheeseburger*
cheeseburger cheeseburger
outside the window because Sarah
says it sounds like it sings *cheeseburger*
cheeseburger cheeseburger
Sarah sounds a lot like she's getting away
with most everything while
she looks through the window while
she works at her desk
while she listens while I imagine her
whistling while she works
Sarah who maybe if we were young
in the 50's I would have
called a bird a nice bird a beauty of a bird
something like that or maybe
look at that little birdie over there
I might've said at a carnival somewhere
in Kansas to some fool
fool enough to be friends with me but we
aren't living in the 50s
and south Louisiana isn't any place
like Kansas so to get started
convincing her to marry me I said *please*
come to this Halloween reading
I'll be dolled up channeling
Dorothy Parker at a bar downtown

and now that was nearly
nine years ago so I guess it worked
but now we never mention
Baton Rouge with all its warring corner
drugstores where the young
couples have long ago stopped crowding
around red boxes planted
all over town for the newest movie
about the oldest past times
instead we keep on like everyone
pretending we're different that we'll live
forever if we just keep singing
like a couple of new birds
with our beaks full of *cheeseburger*
cheeseburger cheeseburger

one last hurricane party in nc

long before we fly away from everything
our everything flooded our *coup*
of causeways, levees, and rougarou
so it seems only appropriate
on our one evening together
before leaving the country
we get a hurricane party in nc
rain thick and theatrical
like its presence had been paid for
a professional mourner storm
gathered above a united states
and brobaby wake of sorts
avoiding premature threats
to jump into the grave
(we remind ourselves
we climbed out of one)
I went downtown to replace
my brother's glasses—gratefully
the only thing lost in another
average pizza delivery mugging—
then the wailing started
so we rushed back to the house
(after buying bottles of booze)
like any good louisianian knows to do
we also made a second line parade
during a soft spell found in a crevice between clouds
noisily marching with both families, dogs, and umbrellas
to discover and admire a lightning tree

brought down blackened a block away
returning we all porch sat for a beer or two
new rain curtains straining the leftover light of day
angeliki looked comfortable swinging
and playing dress up with finn
the hounds resigned themselves
to their spots on the floor
while the rest of us began reminiscing
ever-ascending in our flight of festivities
this wasn't our first party
where the lights went out
singing and dancing in front
of all our books to the boss
sarah gracefully pulls out the candles
—duly making their lighting and placing
an impromptu performance—
while I prepare a champagne toast
shippy insists on starting a corpse
so we pass the glasses and pen
scribbling and drawing flickers as if
it was our amalgam's last stand

VII. LIVING PAST THE INVISIBLE

corona cooler

my parents have had this ivory green-lid, hard shell
handle-locking cooler probably since the seventies
I have wish fulfillment dreams about filling it

perpetually in past garages being prepared
or in the trunk teeming with tea, ice, soda cans
a staple while driving errands around the south
as my step-mother   god bless her soul
to this day and with no exaggeration
considers making groceries a commission
to visit no less than five stores

especially reliant on it for our road trips
we used to drive to camden, charleston, myrtle beach
up I-95 to connecticut for christmas
packing sandwiches, spreads, string cheese
you name it   but it was the family cooler
              meaning little to no beer
(until I got a hold of it in adolescence)

it's curious how many things get lost between
two divorces   three children   three to five moves
(depending on who's counting)
a first born male's curfew abuse
after being dragged to idaho
in the midst of high school
but that cooler still rides

(I have another relic
a soft heineken six pack satchel
my college girlfriend gifted me
from the amsterdam factory
that made it through 18 mardi gras
and fatedly found its way home
to the netherlands(—even after
a few months stint with the shipmans)!

I walk to the cooler's corner
in my parents' garage
even now as I type across the atlantic
notice how the lid is upside down
placed ajar to ensure evaporation
still the shell's integrity is supreme
the lid's green no less olive
the ivory bottom a softer cream
like out-of-tune piano keys
that cooler sashays to me in my sleep

I count the ways to get it here opposite
to how the media now counts the corona cases
per country and how everyone crusades
about where you're from
and where you've been
facemasks first   online auctions
asians wearing out of consideration
even started appearing on the faces
of public sculptures
handshaking bans

airports and ubers abandoned
conferences canceled
weddings   honeymoons   postponed
universities suspending live instruction
sporting events played in closed stadiums
this morning's viral video
shelby county parents
spraying their kids with lysol in the street
the pickup line turned picket line
one woman all decked out
with thick yellow raincoat and grocery bags
an impromptu hazmat suit
for living past the invisible

despite the media's all-day dose of virus
in which they can't seem to decide
if cases or deaths are more worth reporting
over a week into quarantine
and we haven't been armed with real information about biology
or protocol for treatment besides calling our family doctor
if we have a fever and staying at home for two weeks
(who's ice chest in a city is full enough to last that long?)
then what? you either die or you get over the covid?
care to disclose any long-term effects to us?
from what little I know viruses—like coolers—can last
a lifetime and can store many a thing deep inside them
but since all probability indicates this beer-named plague
is not grand enough to cause the end of times
I'm going to return to my cold plot to import this heirloom
to europe for summer excursions to scheveningen

Spring Quarantine

I wondered if my wife snapped
a quick pic of me
sprawled out beside her on the lawn.

It seemed like an opportunity
to get a good shot.

Legs stretched. Booted feet
crossed. Hands tucked
behind my head, tilting the grey
Carhartt hat

down over my eyes to block
what little sun there was.
Last year's *Best American Poetry*
open face-down on my chest.

Quarantine—the pithy Instagram
caption could read—
or maybe *The Poet Dozes Away
Another Apocalypse*.

I wanted her to snap
the pic, but I didn't want to say it.

I didn't want a single word to fall
from a single mouth.
Not only because I wanted her

to think I was asleep. I just
wanted her to know—somewhere
in her beautiful blood.

I just wanted
something to happen—to fall
naturally into place.

We're not talking anyway. Not
about anything other
than COVID-19 anyway—singing
its monstrous aria, or trying to
over the sui generis
notes of spring, which is

why I was on the lawn (I remind
only myself) in the first place.

I had to face the facts. Yesterday
was the first day
of spring. And last night brought
the first spring rain.

Before my wife sat beside me
she was on the porch—
the light wind holding her
like a kind of triage
for what the wind might prescribe
in whatever crueler months
come to stumble us.

When she saw me she drifted
down to the damp grass
with her stack of ungraded papers.

I still don't know if she snapped
a pic on her phone—of me
pretending to sleep. I'll ask her
when we're talking again
about anything that resembles
anything again.

Now, hours later, seems like days.
She's on the phone
with her brother, checking in
to see how his business in Maine
is faring against the virus.

They spend a long time talking
about the repeated failures
of their father and older brother
to make amends.
Then my wife mentions
their grandfather, a WWII hero.

He was someone, she says
who saw the end
of the world, then lived past it.

Now it's raining again—harder
somehow, because Mark
our neighbor and friend, is back
from visiting his mother
at the hospital. I wonder

if it's safe to be around him
now—now as I'm reading a text
he just sent, about
rethinking our *buddy status*
during quarantine.

I wonder what iniquity will mean
tomorrow, the third day
of spring. I wonder
if my wife will snap, or me.
Try to forget how to begin
any sentence with *when* or *wind*.

The rain's stopped for now.
I need to brave the store
for bread and beer. First I'll move
the box of sidewalk chalk
from the driveway.

I don't want to ruin one
of our daughter's distractions.

Her sun is already a yellow smear
across the concrete—
a broken yoke left to gather
an army of ants—
and I'm no war hero.

ride again

time will show you its tell
in the love letters of an outlaw
kept next to your breast

the ones
that demand
tall bottles
and pens
in saloons
chief
in company
of fools
making our marks
with the only weapon
ever able to deny
laws man-made
and natural

our first hands
we lay large blinds
against distance
go all in
on a bluff

the action
of friends
writers
lovers

a trifecta
at the track
wearing our lucky
go-to-hell hats

then we find the real stakes
to our wagers we place
with our very lives

the who
what
and where
of the ride
with a why
so often found
only in hindsight

like the perfect type of light
you need to detect it's raining
during the day sometimes
but then again
it could just be your eyes—
old accomplices

The News on the Corner

it's difficult to describe the noise
of news on constant cycle
eternally   blooming in the bottom

corner of my computer screen
but I don't have to   you   know what
it sounds like   like

mario eating a mushroom   like
a coin dropped into a slot like a voice
that doesn't know what

language to speak   that doesn't know
what language is   that is   lost in a sea
of its own making of waves   of its own

making waves that are
our fears our masks our latex gloves
gripped around the splintering wood

of our protest signs of our protests   of us
protesting because every   gust of wind
is reminiscent of a lover   leaving us

for a country burying   the hatchet with
all the hatchets then digging up all
the hatchets with hatchets   till the dirt is

packed like silence is buried
is the language of
         the corner of heart it falls out

speaks something   we want
to hear   we want   to believe
no more knees pressed into necks

no more shooting or tweets about
shooting no more presidential policing
                               no more

noise blooming like loud dark
mushrooms darkening
loudly at the bottom of   our screens

like the opposite   of cartoons
or video games   lost to the sea of dreams
black kids can't grow up   to become

because of us eternally us
failing to describe corners coined
which is all to say   my eyes my ears

are strapped   to you   my friend
so rejoicing   I am   to be
to get away   with   everything

to share this sacred space is to hold
ourselves in the dark   to press against
the noise   the terrible

novelty of light   to tell every story
to get away
         with   nothing

if not a line   break

~getting away with everything

follow the yellow bit inroad

stockpiling serendipity
in a server cave
of technocracy
like it was sarin
and we've got
an oz plot planned
but the era of terror
got too stale to sell
so now there's
a new normal to swallow
making bygone terrorist threat levels
look like paint by numbers
for world travel as we are now
more or less embargoed
contained to a dull panic
pandemic 8 weeks reborn
alone, unformed ironically
by being over-informed despite
less ado about everything
big data eats the little
isolation worm afraid
of where the sidewalk begins
or just going to the store
ricocheting to the voids
of the aisles with more
end times supplies on your person
than even purchasing
vices and devices little

more than morning chores
I've taken to fondly singeing
my bare hand on the teapot
to taste a past life
spoons are the only utensils
I continue to use
not for measuring my life
but for devouring the jot of stock one can
still render from three millennia old marrow
and when I can muster the courage
to expound upon my jettisoned position
I chronicle my life of limited rebellion
crouching towards the desire to see
an even fuller spectrum
hopping fences   peaking on mountains
risking insanity for sanity
willingly jigsawing the heart
to reassemble with anyone that fascinates
me and cares enough to abandon
their own assured understandings
for adventures full as moon
over dense cities itching
to crawl with pleasure again
    push past forces of the state
that have never represented
interest besides their golden own
not that I haven't striven to
become more than mere anarchy
a pusherman of language
and the experience to wield it

evermore flirting with the outer rims
of rhyme going as far as publishing *fuck poems*
yet partnered up with a 9 to 5   2 mortgages
actually contemplating pushing a stroller
and definitely for the first time
since the pinch of adolescence
a more sober than not disposition
I debate how much I have settled
an extent I may have hurled farther
at the expense of my liberty or life itself
I did flee a country I could no longer bear
enabling and intermittently I agonize
about what that makes me some eves
more of a daybreak dreamer
than a resistance deserter
others a civil disobedient
ghost sheltering in a library
by working with silence and white space
even before we all had to shelter in place
certainly an expert at starting from scratch
I speak my mind when I care to   which is less and less
and right now—world over—there is an invisible plague
which begs the declaration we will all die in any language
one way or several so there's really no getting away
but on a page or in a virtual space   deprived of
the senses that   on occasion
make rotting for eternity almost bearable
although just beginning to code
I know now that our machines
promise to exceed us

as the only lifetime learners
that can ignore death
maybe we should listen
a little more closely
to their songs
I heard a good one yesterday
claim in its outro
we want revolution
constant change
give to everyone
food and clothes
kill the government kill the system
kill the government kill the system
if that's the AI revolution sapiens have
been so afraid of let's
follow the update upstage

on my 37th year and yet another day around the sun

gas grenades and rubber bullets win yet another day
riots and racism protests burn in the divided states furnace
after yet another series of executions by the police
men and women caught red-handed for being black
in the streets or in their homes fast asleep
my country is suffering a pandemic, a recession and
is so divided it can't even take a breath of the least-polluted skies
it's tasted since before the industrial revolution
back home between protests
my friends board up windows
ready the generators as yet another
hurricane looms on louisiana
so far away I reach further within
nowhere near comprehending
america's sick in the head
as the old folks used to say
some now probably repeat
as if simple bigotry could save them from a plague
sickened by their lack of surplus
without identifying the correct culprits
like welfare money is better off buried
even after civil rights and the hippies
the powers at be managed to slip us
america's true favorite drug: ignorance
hey greatest generation
or everyone wearing bloody caps
the black bodies that made it great the first time
can take no more abuse

it's not a threat to you
to eliminate the centuries-standing death threat on blacks
sheathe your assault rifle and park the tanks
we're just trying not to get here yet again
yet another birthday sentiment
when we usually make a wish or two for the impossible
bargain days   a mad dash backwards from the grave
the earliest hide and seek we never win
but blue on black death daily...
and although I'm not out in the streets dodging police
to make a statement of solidarity
I violently punch keys that know no answers
the letters are my only black neighbors
they are the only way I can join the drumline for justice
determined forms that build the page black and permanent
as the night and the fears we steady there are infinite

An American Vigil

It is not forbidden yet   to play the jester
so the boss man wears his "o-*so*-contemporary!" cap
    to the obligatory office party;
    you know
    the one:

the sad American red   snapback shaped
                     like an oubliette—

wild as the masses   at half-mast;
strange
as the bigotry sweating the need
now to hide beneath it—for the first time—
     its infinite strands.

Let us consider one story: Every strand a seashore
disappearing.   Every bit
of stubble a spike—a blade contending
         ownership of sand and retracting
equal rights
         like shadows
        cast over shadows.

A literal littoral   foaming white
        flooded with blacked-out ghosts
of black bodies is not
a metaphorical leap.   We

born betrothed to the past　　　　　see what is lost
in the long　　　　　　divorce
　　　　　　　　　　　because it's caught
　　　　　　　　　　　on film.

　　　　　I suppose it's alright to tell you—
　　　　　I suppose you already know—
　　　　　something the opposite
　　　　　of Wordsworthian
　　　　　has my tongue by
　　　　　its pincers.

So I tell the jokes I know to the people I know
backed into the corners I know.　　　　　Here

I shake my fist　　　　　rattle
the glassy ice disappearing　　　　　and begin

disappearing

toward the bar. I am an ocean
falling on the walkable world.

I might as well grow wings because　　I know how
to fool everyone—could force fun from an egg cup
　　　　　　　　　　　　　(if you have one handy).

　　　　　I can like a nest fashion a laugh
　　　　　out of white feathers
　　　　　and white sky.

As in sharp against. As in dull against.
As in the screwed up punchline. As in
the usual disappointments. As in

the big boss man   clamoring around
the obligatory office party   pretending
everything

        above / below
            the unbroken bill
of his numbly contemporary cap

              isn't falling
                  from the sky.

If we can cast an eye
toward the deluge
as even the horizon grows small and dim

sinking itself into the sea as if into a dusty corner's
forgotten spill—
if we can
reimagine a shore   its sun fastened
to another rise—
            stand firm at its water's edge

    maybe any voice   backed
into any corner

won't cease to speak   until the sky ceases
to fall.

    The sky is never finished
        so nothing is.

wounded soldier

wanted to write
you a poem
instead I have to
paint a porch

there are fish guts
everywhere
and my heart's
on the subway
floor rolling
around with
the other empties

spilling over

acknowledgments

Much obliged to the editors of the publications in which versions of the following poems first appeared:

"Solastalgia" in *North Carolina Literary Review*

"This Morning" and "Here Comes the Rain" in *Comstock Review*

"drive thru confessional, unframed" and "An American Vigil" *in Moss Trill*

"Time Travel" in *Naugatuck River Review*

"Spring Quarantine" and "Sharing a Smoke" in *Unlikely Stories*

"Now When I Am" in *3 Elements Review*

"lurking in the glow" and "chronic chthonic disorder" in *Expanded Field*

"everything possible" under the title "no one was harmed in the making of this poem" in *DREICH Mag*

"my blur flew from puddle to puddle" *in E•ratio*

"honestly" in *Mardi Gras Zine* by Lucky Bean Poetry Press and NOLA DNA

"Jack's Ashes" and "Family Reunion at the Hunting Lodge" in *antonym*

"precarious nothings" in *Sledgehammer*

shout-outs

Deepest thanks to our publisher and editor, Jonathan Penton, for gracing us with a stage for Act II. Your keen direction and endless patience have allowed us to leave nothing waiting in the wings.

Thanks to our friends and families for suffering us and mending us.

Special thanks to Beth Ann Fennelly, Kenning JP García, and Bill Lavender for lending words to our words.

And very special thanks to Sarah K. Jackson, Angeliki Sioli, and Rosalyn Spencer for the love that lets us be privileged, lucky, and Unlikely so-and-so's.

And again, and always—thank you, Michelle! We finished this on your birthday and felt your guiding hand the whole way.

about the authors

Vincent A. Cellucci wrote *Absence Like Sun* (Lavender Ink, 2019) and *An Easy Place / To Die* (CityLit Press, 2011). He edited *Fuck Poems an exceptional anthology* (Lavender Ink, 2012). He also has two collaborative titles: *come back river* (Finishing Line Press, 2014), Bengali-English translation collaborations with artist and poet Debangana Banerjee, and *_a ship on the line* (Unlikely Books, 2014), which was a finalist for the Eric Hoffer Award. Vincent performed "Diamonds in Dystopia," an interactive poetry web app at SXSW in 2017, and the poem was anthologized in *Best American Experimental Writing 2018*. After writing and living it up in Louisiana for 18 carnivals, he moved to the Netherlands to experience sinking some place new. He haunts the TU Delft Library.

Christopher Shipman is the author of *The Movie My Murderer Makes: Season II* (The Cupboard), coauthor of *Super Poems II* (Kattywompus Press), and coauthor of *Keats is Not the Problem* (Lavender Ink). His work appears in journals such as *Cimarron Review*, *PANK*, *Pedestal*, *Plume*, *Salt Hill*, *Spork Press*, and *TENDERLOIN*, among many others. He is the author or coauthor of five books and four chapbooks. His poem, "The Three-Year Crossing," was a winner of the 2015 Big Bridges Prize, judged by Alice Quinn. *_a ship on the line* (2015), coauthored with Vincent A. Cellucci, was a finalist for the Eric Hoffer Award. Shipman lives in Greensboro, NC with his partner Sarah K. Jackson and his daughter Finn, where he teaches literature and creative writing at New Garden Friends School and plays drums in the band The Goodbye Horses. Learn more at CShipmanWriting.com.

other titles by Vincent A. Cellucci

Absence Like Sun (Lavender Ink, 2019)

_a ship on the line (Unlikely Books, 2014)

come back river (Finishing Line Press, 2014)

ed. *Fuck Poems an exceptional anthology* (Lavender Ink, 2012)

An Easy Place / To Die (CityLit, 2011)

other titles by Christopher Shipman

Super Poems II w/ Brent Dixon and Kristen Foster (Kattywompus Press, 2020)

The Movie My Murderer Makes: Season II (The Cupboard, 2018)

Keats is Not the Problem w/ Brett Evans (Lavender Ink, 2017)

Cat Poems: Wompus Tales and a Play of Despair (Kattywompus Press, 2015)

_a ship on the line w/ Vincent A. Cellucci (Unlikely Books, 2014)

T. Rex Parade w/ Brett Evans (Lavender Ink, 2014)

The Movie My Murderer Makes (The Cupboard, 2014)

Super Poems w/ Dewitt Brinson (Kattywompus Press, 2012)

Romeo's Ugly Nose w/ Benjamin Cockfield (Allography, 2012)

Human-Carrying Flight Technology (Blaze Vox, 2012)

recent titles from Unlikely Books

fata morgana by Joel Chace

Typescenes by Rodney A. Brown

Political AF: A Rage Collection by Tara Campbell

The Deepest Part of Dark by Anne Elezebeth Pluto

Swimming Home by Kayla Rodney

Manything by dan raphael

Citizen Relent by Jeff Weddle

The Mercy of Traffic by Wendy Taylor Carlisle

Cantos Poesia by David E. Matthews

Left Hand Dharma: New and Selected Poems by Belinda Subraman

Apocalyptics by C. Derick Varn

Pachuco Skull with Sombrero: Los Angeles, 1970 by Lawrence Welsh

Monolith by Anne McMillen (Second Edition)

When Red Blood Cells Leak by Anne McMillen (Second Edition)

My Hands Were Clean by Tom Bradley (Second Edition)

anonymous gun. by Kurtice Kucheman (Second Edition)

Soy solo palabras but wish to be a city by Leon De la Rósa, illustrated by Gui.ra.ga7 (Second Edition)

Ghazals 1-59 and Other Poems by Sheila E. Murphy and Michelle Greenblatt

ASHES AND SEEDS by Michelle Greenblatt

_a ship on the line by Vincent A. Cellucci and Christopher Shipman

www.ingramcontent.com/pod-product-compliance
Lightning Source LLC
Chambersburg PA
CBHW080224100526
44583CB00020BA/2556